INDIAN
HISTORICAL RESEARCHES

THE KESAVA TEMPLE AT BELUR

INDIAN
HISTORICAL RESEARCHES

THE KESAVA TEMPLE AT BELUR

INDIAN TEMPLE ARCHITECTURE

R. NARASIMHACHAR

GYAN

Published by

GYAN

Gyan Publishing House
5, Ansari Road
Daryaganj, New Delhi-110002
Phone: 011-47034999, 9811692060
E-mail: books@gyanbooks.com

Distribution Network
gyanbooks.com
India, USA, Canada, UK, Australia, France

ISBN : 978-81-212-2798-8 (HB)
First Published, 1911

2nd Impression 2021

Printed at: Gyan Press, Delhi.

Indian
Historical Researches
The Kesava Temple At Belur
Author: R. Narasimhachar

INTRODUCTORY NOTE.

THE present work forms the second of the Mysore Archæological Series: *Architecture and Sculpture in Mysore*, and deals with the Kesava temple at Belur, one of the most exquisite specimens of the Hoysala style of architecture, built by the Hoysala king Vishnuvardhana in A. D. 1117. The Kesava temple at Somanathapur, treated of in the first monograph of this Series, is a *trikutachala* or three-celled structure, while the subject of the present monograph consists of only one cell, though sorrounded by several temples, shrines and subsidiary buildings, and, being older than the other by nearly one hundred and fifty years, may be looked upon as one of the earlier examples of the Hoysala style. According to Fergusson it combines constructive propriety with exuberant decoration to an extent not often surpassed in any part of the world.

To do anything like justice to the marvellous elaboration and beauty of the details of this gem of architecture hundreds of plates are necessary. For the purpose of this short monograph, however, only some of the most striking features have been selected and the temple is illustrated by forty-five plates. The illustrations have been prepared by Mr. T. Namassivayam Pillai, the Photographer and Draughtsman of my Office.

The list of the artistic buildings of the Hoysala and Dravidian styles in Mysore given in the first monograph has now been enlarged to some extent by the addition of some more monuments of the two styles brought to light by recent exploration. Though by no means exhaustive, it is sufficient to give an idea of the richness of Mysore in these artistic treasures.

It only remains for me to express my thanks to scholars and the press for their appreciative notices of my Monograph on the Kesava temple at Somanathapur.

BANGALORE,
JUNE 1919.

R. NARASIMHACHAR.

v

PROVISIONAL LIST OF ARTISTIC BUILDINGS OF THE HOYSALA AND DRAVIDIAN STYLES IN MYSORE.

Those that are marked with an asterisk are more or less in a ruinous condition.

HOYSALA.

Temple	Place	Period	Reign	Remarks
1. Basavesvara	Tonachi	C. 1047	Vinayaditya ...	...
2. Mallinatha-basti*	Angadi	C. 1050	do ...	...
3. Kedaresvara	Belgami	C. 1060	do ...	Triple.
4. Tripurantaka*	do	1070	do ...	Double.
5. Kaitabhesvara	Kuppatur	C. 1070	do ...	...
6. Adinatha-basti	Chikka Hanasoge	C. 1090	do ...	Triple.
7. Lakshmidevi	Dodda Gaddavalli	1113	Vishnuvardhana	Quadruple
8. Kesava	Belur	1117	do ...	...
9. Kappe-Chennigaraya ...	do	C. 1117	do ...	Double.
10. Vira-Narayana	do	C. 1117	do ...	...
11. Kirti-Narayana	Talkad	1117	do ...	...
12. Dharmesvara	Grama	1123	do ...	...
13. Kesava	do	C. 1123	do ...	...
14. Narasimha	do	C. 1123	do ...	...
15. Kesava	Marale	1130	do ...	...
16. Siddhesvara	do	1130	do ...	...
17. Parsvanatha-basti	Halebid	1133	do ...	...
18. Hoysalesvara	do	C. 1141	Narasimha I ...	Double.
19. Jain basti*	Cholasandra	1145	do ...	Triple.
20. Kesava*	Honnavara	1149	do ...	...
21. Nagesvara*	Nidugal-durga	C. 1150	do ...	...
22. Parsvanatha-basti	Heggere	1160	do ...	...
23. Isvara	Anekonda	C. 1160	do ...	...
24. Kesava	Dharmapura	1163	do ...	...
25. Do	Hullekere	1163	do ...	...
26. Hoysalesvara*	Tenginagatta	C. 1163	do ...	...
27. Narayana*	Suttur	1169	do ...	...

HOYSALA—*contd.*

TEMPLE	PLACE	PERIOD	REIGN	REMARKS
28. Somesvara	Suttur	C. 1169	Narasimha I ...	Triple.
29. Kesava	Nagamangala	C. 1170	do ...	do
30. Brahmesvara	Kikkeri	1171	do ...	...
31. Buchesvara	Koramangala	1173	do ...	...
32. Akkana-basti	Sravana Belgola ...	1182	Ballala II ...	...
33. Amritesvara	Amritapura ...	1196	do ...	...
34. Singesvara*	Hebbalalu	1200	do ...	...
35. Santinatha-basti	Jinanathapura	C. 1200	do ...	...
36. Mahalingesvara*	Mavuttanhalli	C. 1200	do ...	Triple.
37. Chattesvara*	Chatchattanhalli	C. 1200	do ...	do
38. Trimurti	Bandalike	C. 1200	do ...	do
39. Anekal	do	C. 1200	do ...	do
40. Kodanda-Rama	Hirimagalur	C. 1200	do ...	...
41. Siddhesvara	Kodakani	C. 1200	do ...	...
42. Mallesvara	Huliyar	C. 1200	do ...	...
43. Virabhadra	Grama	C. 1200	do ...	Double.
44. Andal	Belur	C. 1200	do ...	...
45. Sankaresvara*	do	C. 1200	do ...	...
46. Kesava*	Angadi	C. 1200	do ...	...
47. Santinatha-basti*	Bandalike	C. 1204	do ...	...
48. Kirti-Narayana	Heragu	1218	do ...	...
49. Kedaresvara	Halebid	1219	do ...	...
50. Virabhadra	do	C. 1220	do ...	...
51. Sahasrakuta-basti	Arsikere	1220	do ...	...
52. Isvara	do	C. 1220	do ...	...
53. Do	Nanditavare	C. 1220	do ...	...
54. Harihara	Harihar	1224	Narasimha II ...	...
55. Mule-Singesvara*	Bellur	1224	do ...	Triple.
56. Kallesvara*	Heggere	1232	do ...	...
57. Galagesvara*	do	C. 1232	do ...	...
58. Somesvara	Harnhalli	1234	do ...	...
59. Kesava	do	C. 1234	do ...	...
60. Mallikarjuna	Basaral	1235	do ...	Triple.
61. Lakshmi-Narasimha ...	Nuggihalli	1249	Somesvara ...	do

HOYSALA—*concld.*

Temple	Place	Period	Reign	Remarks
62. Sadasiva	Nuggihalli	C. 1249	Somesvara ...	...
63. Lakshmi-Narasimha ...	Javagal	C. 1250	do ...	Triple.
64. Isvara*	Budanur	C. 1250	do ...	...
65. Padmanabha*	do	C. 1250	do ...	...
66. Panchalinga	Govindanhalli	C. 1250	do ...	Quintuple
67. Kesava*	Nagalapura	C. 1250	do ...	...
68. Kedaresvara*	do	C. 1250	do ...	...
69. Mallesvara*	Hulikal	C. 1250	do ...	...
70. Kesava	Tandaga	C. 1250	do ...	...
71. Lakshmi-Narayana	Hosaholalu	C. 1250	do ...	Triple.
72. Kesava	Aralaguppe	C. 1250	do ...	...
73. Do	Turuvekere	C. 1260	Narasimha III ...	...
74. Mule-Sankaresvara	do	C. 1260	do ...	...
75. Yoga-Madhava	Settikere	1261	do ...	Triple.
76. Kesava	Somanathapur	1268	do ...	do
77. Madhavaraya	Bellur	C. 1270	do ...	do
78. Lakshmi-Narasimha ...	Hole-Narsipur	C. 1270	do ...	do
79. Do	Vignasante	1286	do ...	do
80. Balalingesvara*	do	C. 1286	do ...	...
81. Lakshmikanta	Hedatale	C. 1292	Ballala III ...	...
82. Nagaresvara*	do	C. 1292	do ...	...

DRAVIDIAN.

Temple	Place	Period	Reign	Remarks
1. Nandisvara	Nandi	C. 800	Govinda III ...	...
2. Lakshmanesvara, etc. ...	Avani	C. 940	Bira-Nolamba ...	...
3. Chamundaraya-basti ...	Sravana Belgola ...	C. 980	Rachamalla IV ...	...
4. Kallesvara	Aralaguppe	C. 1091	Tribhuvanamalla	...
5. Muktinathesvara*	Binnamangala	C. 1100	Kulottunga-Chola	...
6. Vaidyesvara	Talkad	C. 1100	do ...	...
7. Panchakuta-basti*	Kambadahalli ...	C. 1120	Vishnuvardhana	...
8. Narasimha	Agara	C. 1120	do ...	..
9. Gangadharesvara	Kaidala	1151	Narasimha I ...	...
10. Amara-Narayana	Kaivara	C. 1250	Selvandai-Devar	...

DRAVIDIAN—concld.

Temple	Place	Period	Reign	Remarks
11. Somesvara	Kurudumale	C. 1250	Ilavanji-Vasudeva-raya.	...
12. Do	Nidugal-durga	1232	Ganesvara-Deva	...
13. Do	Kolar	C. 1300	Ballala III ...	...
14. Arkesvara	Hale-Alur	C. 1300	do ...	...
15. Vidyasankara	Sringeri	C. 1356	Bukka I ...	...
16. Mallikarjuna	Pankajanhalli	C. 1510	Krishna-Deva-Raya.	...
17. Aghoresvara	Ikkeri	C. 1560	Sankanna-Nayaka I	...
18. Ranganatha	Rangasthala	C. 1600	Palegars ...	...
19. Gaurisvara	Yelandur	1654	Mudda-Raja ...	...
20. Nilakanthesvara	Jambitige	1738	Somasekhara-Nayaka II.	...

LIST OF PLATES.

ARCHITECTURE AND SCULPTURE IN MYSORE.

No. II.

THE KESAVA TEMPLE AT BELUR.

BELUR, the head-quarters of the taluk of the same name in the Hāssan District of the Mysore State, is situated in 13° 10′ N. and 75° 55′ E. on the right bank of the Yagachi or Badari, the chief tributary of the river Hēmāvati, which it joins at Gorūr in the Hāssan Taluk. It is 28 miles to the south-west of Bāṇāvār, a railway station on the Bangalore-Poona line, and 24 miles to the north-west of Hāssan on the Hāssan-Chikmagaḷūr road. In old inscriptions it is named Beluhūr and occasionally Vēlāpura, the latter name occurring mostly in later inscriptions and literature. It was once the capital (*rājadhāni*) of the Hoysaḷa kings: Ballāḷa I (1100-1106) ruled the kingdom from the capital Beluhūr,[1] and Vishṇuvardhana, his younger brother, ruled the kingdom from the great city Vēlāpura in 1117[2] and from the capital Beluhūr in 1123.[3] Owing to its sanctity the place is described in later inscriptions as the modern earthly Vaikuṇṭha (*abhinava-kshōṇī-Vaikuṇṭha*),[4] the great holy seat in the three worlds (*trilōka-mahā-sthānaṃ*) and the southern Benares (*dakshiṇa-Vārāṇasi*).[5] Some time after the destruction by the Muhummadans of Dōrasamudra or Haḷebīḍ, the celebrated Hoysaḷa capital situated about 10 miles to the east of Bēlūr, the latter continued as the capital of the Bēlūr kingdom which was conferred

[1] *Epigraphia Carnatica*, IV, Nāgamangala 32; and *Ibid.*, VI, Chikmagaḷūr 160.

[2] *Ibid.*, V, Bēlūr 58 and 71.

[3] *Ibid.*, Hāssan 116.

[4] Mēlkōṭe in the Seringapatam Taluk is also known as *bhūlōka-Vaikuṇṭha*, Vaikuṇṭha being the abode of Vishṇu.

[5] *Ep. Car.*, V, Bēlūr 4.

by the Vijayanagar king Kṛishṇa-Dēva-Rāya (1509-1529) on Era-Kṛishṇappa-Nāyaka, the bearer of his *haḍapa* or betel-bag, whose successors ruled over the principality for nearly two centuries. In 1645 the Bēlūr kingdom was overrun by the Ikkēri chief Śivappa-Nāyaka and bestowed by him on Śrī-Ranga-Rāya, the fugitive king of Vijayanagar who had fled to him for refuge. But in accordance with a treaty concluded between Mysore and Ikkēri in 1694 a portion of the principality was ceded to the Bēlūr chiefs and the rest annexed to Mysore.

The Kēśava temple at Bēlūr is one of the most exquisite specimens of the Hoysaḷa style of architecture. From the fine inscription[1] on the east wall to the left of the north entrance of the central hall (Plate XLIV) we learn that the Hoysaḷa king Vishṇuvardhana caused the temple to be erected and set up the god Vijaya-Nārāyaṇa in it in A.D. 1117. There is also a copper plate inscription[2] in the temple which is similar in contents to the stone inscription mentioned above and gives the same date. Recently an inscription in the form of an *anushtubh* verse was discovered on the pedestal of the god, which states that king Vishṇu caused to be made the image of Vijaya-Nārāyaṇa. It will thus be seen that the god is named Vijaya-Nārāyaṇa in the old inscriptions, though popularly known as Kēśava. According to tradition this temple was erected by Vishṇuvardhana to commemorate his conversion by the celebrated Vaishṇava apostle Rāmānujāchārya from the Jaina to the Vaishṇava faith. It is also stated that Rāmānujāchārya deputed his sister's son and disciple Mudaliyāṇḍān to assist at the consecration ceremony. Tradition also attributes to Vishṇuvardhana the consecration on one and the same occasion of five images of Nārāyaṇa (*pañcha-Nārāyaṇa-pratishṭhe*) at different places, namely, Bēlūr, Talkāḍ, Mēlkōṭe, Toṇṇūr and Gadag, though according to one account Guṇḍlupēṭ comes in for the honor instead of Gadag. As we saw above, there is epigraphical confirmation of the tradition with regard to Bēlūr. A few years ago, during the excavations that were conducted around the Kīrti-Nārāyaṇa temple at Talkāḍ, a Tamil inscription was disclosed on the basement of the temple recording that Vishṇuvardhana, having rooted out Adiyamān, the Chōla viceroy, took possession of Talkāḍ and set up the god

[1] *Ep. Car.*, V, Bēlūr 58.

[2] Bēlūr 71

Kīrti-Nārāyaṇa in it in A.D. 1117.[1] So, the tradition with regard to Talkāḍ is also borne out by epigraphical evidence. We have to await further research with regard to the remaining places, each of which has an old temple dedicated to Nārāyaṇa.

The Kēśava temple is situated in a court measuring 443′ 6″ by 396′ and enclosed by a high wall, surrounded by several temples, minor shrines, *maṇṭapas* or halls, and subsidiary buildings (Plate II). Plate I gives a view from the south of some of the buildings in the enclosure. The temple faces east and has two *mahādvāras* or outer gates in the eastern front, of which the one to the north is surmounted by a lofty *gōpura* or tower. The other gate, which is practically closed, is known as Āne-bāgilu or the Elephant's Gate. The Kēśava temple measures 178′ by 156′ and stands on a terrace, about 3 feet high, which closely follows the contour of the structure. Plate III gives the south view of the temple and Plate IV the north view. The building consists of a *garbha-griha* or adytum, a *sukhanāsi* or vestibule, and a *navaranga* or central hall which has three entrances on the east (Plate V), south, and north (Plate VI). The south entrance is known as "the Friday entrance" (*Śukravāra-bāgilu*) and the north, as "the Heavenly entrance" (*Svargada-bāgilu*). On the jambs of the east doorway (Plate VII) are sculptured Manmatha and his wife Rati; on those of the south, Hanumān and Garuḍa; and on those of the north, female chauri-bearers. The pediments have a projecting panel with a figure of Garuḍa, above which, flanked by *makaras*, we have on the east Narasimha killing the demon Hiraṇyakaśipu, on the south Varāha killing the demon Hiraṇyāksha, and on the north Kēśava. The north and south pediments are carved also on the back.

Beginning at the sides of the east doorway and extending beyond the north and south doorways up to the outer wall of the *sukhanāsi*, runs a *jagati* or railed parapet, on which are sculptured in succession from the bottom the following horizontal friezes: (1) elephants, (2) cornice with bead work surmounted by *simha-lalāṭas* or lions' heads at intervals, (3) scroll work with figures in every convolution, (4) another cornice with bead work, (5) small figures, mostly female, in projecting ornamental niches with intervening figures of Yakshas seated inward; (6) delicately carved figures, mostly female, between pilasters; (7) eaves with bead work with a thick

[1] *Mysore Archæological Report* for 1912, paras 22 and 83.

1*

creeper running along the edge of the upper slope adorned with miniature turrets, lions and beautifully carved tiny figures; and (8) a rail containing figures, sometimes indecent, in panels between double columns surmounted by an ornamental band. It is not known why the moulding above the elephant frieze is left blank all round the temple. Plate VIII shows all the friezes and Plate IX exhibits the railed parapet on an enlarged scale from the second frieze upwards. The rail to the right of the east entrance illustrates briefly the story of the Mahābhārata up to the Śalya-parva: Bhīma is represented as worshipping Gaṇapati, and Duryōdhana as falling unwittingly at the feet of Kṛishṇa, his throne tumbling down by Kṛishṇa pressing his foot against the earth (Plate IX). Further on the frieze on the creeper (7) shows briefly scenes from the Rāmāyaṇa. The same frieze exhibits here and there exquisitely carved tiny seated figures playing on musical instruments. Above the rail come pierced stone windows or perforated screens surmounted by the eaves. These are 20 in number, 10 to the right and 10 to the left of the east doorway, running along the walls up to the left and right sides of the south and north doorways. They form a charming feature of this beautiful temple. Ten of them are sculptured with Purāṇic scenes, and the rest decorated with geometrical designs (Plates X, XI and XII). Of the sculptured ones, five of which are to the right and five to the left of the east doorway, some details are given below:—

First screen to the right of the east doorway.—The sculptures on this are said to represent the *darbār* of king Vishṇuvardhana, who built the temple in 1117 (Plate XIII). The top panel has the god Kēśava in the centre flanked by chauri-bearers as well as Hanumān and Garuḍa. The middle panel shows the king seated in the centre with his queen to the left. He holds a sword in the right hand and a flower in the left. Behind the queen stands a female attendant. To the right of the king, a little to the front, are two seated *gurus* or religious teachers, one of them with his hand in the teaching pose, with two disciples at the back. There are also several officers, attendants, etc., in the group. Some of the figures, including the royal couple, have large ear-lobes with ornaments. The bottom panel has rearing lions with riders as also seated lions.

Third screen.—We have on this the representation of the story of Bali, the demon king, making a gift to Vāmana, the Dwarf incarnation of

Vishṇu. The top panel shows Lakshmīnārāyaṇa flanked by Hanumān and Garuḍa. In the middle panel we see Trivikrama in the centre with his uplifted foot which is washed by Brahmā. To his right stands Bali with folded hands, and to his left two figures of Garuḍa, one with folded hands and the other dragging Śukrāchārya, the minister and preceptor of Bali. The lower panel represents Bali's *darbār*, his making the gift, etc.

Eighth screen.—In the top panel we have Lakshmīnārāyaṇa, with attendants as in the first screen. The middle panel shows Kṛishṇa as Kāḷiyamardana or the punisher of the serpent Kāḷiya with two figures with folded hands at the sides, while the lower one represents a music party.

Ninth screen.—The first panel has Vishṇu flanked as usual by Hanumān and Garuḍa. The second shows Śiva seated on Nandi, flanked by Gaṇapati and Subrahmaṇya and further on by warriors holding flags, swords and shields. The third has the *dikpālakas* or regents of the directions Indra to Kubēra seated on their vehicles, while the fourth represents a battle scene.

Tenth screen.—Here we have the representation of the story of Prahlāda (Plate XIV). The centre of the upper panel is occupied by a figure of Lakshmīnārāyaṇa flanked by Garuḍa and another figure which is not Hanumān. The middle panel has a figure of Narasimha killing Hiraṇyakaśipu, with Garuḍa and Hanumān at the sides. The lower panel shows four seated figures of Prahlāda with folded hands undergoing various kinds of torture. Incidentally it may be mentioned here that all the four figures of Prahlāda wear Tenkale *nāmam* on their foreheads. This is of some interest as proving the antiquity of this Śrivaishṇava mark, as we shall see further on that the perforated screens of this temple were caused to be made by Ballāḷa II (1173—1220), the grandson of Vishṇuvardhana.

First screen to the left of the east doorway.—This is mostly similar to the first screen to the right (Plate XV). It is said to represent the *darbār* of king Nārasimha I, the son of Vishṇuvardhana. The top panel shows Yōga-Narasimha flanked by chauri-bearers as well as Hanumān and Garuḍa. The middle panel has the king seated in the centre with his queen to the left. He holds a sword in the right hand and a flower in the left. At the left end are seen three seated figures with folded hands wearing coats. These may represent officers. There are also several attendants in the group. The bottom panel has lions like the first screen to the right.

Fourth screen.—The first panel has a seated figure of Vishṇu, while the second illustrates the story of the churning of the milk ocean.

Seventh screen.—The upper panel has Vishṇu flanked as usual by Hanumān and Garuḍa. The second depicts the killing of Kamsa by Kṛishṇa, while the third delineates his killing the elephant Kuvalayāpīḍa and his contest with the wrestler Chāṇūra. The fourth shows him as playing on the flute, the notes of which are intently listened to not only by the cows but also by the wild beasts.

Ninth screen.—This shows a figure of Ranganātha reclining on a beautifully carved serpent.

Tenth screen.—The top panel has Lakshmīnārāyaṇa flanked by chauri-bearers. In the second we see Hanumān and Garuḍa fighting over what looks like a *linga* placed between them. Both of them have laid their hands on it. The *linga* is split into two halves by the discus of Vishṇu seated above. The combatants seem to have exchanged their head-dresses during the fight: we see Hanumān wearing the crown of Garuḍa.

The pillars at the sides of every screen have on their capitals figures standing out supporting the eaves. These bracket figures, which are mostly female, are wonderful works of art. They are called *madanakai* figures in Kannaḍa. Two of them represent Durgā and three are huntresses, one bearing a bow and the others shooting birds with arrows. Most of the other figures are either dancing or playing on musical instruments or dressing or decorating themselves. Several of them are represented as wearing breeches. Once there were forty of them around the temple, and it is fortunate that only two are now missing. Four of these can be seen on Plate V, four on Plate VI, and two each on Plates XII, XIII and XV. Out of these ten figures, six are shown separately on Plate XVI. Of the 38 figures now standing around the temple, it is interesting to note that 18 are signed images, *i.e.*, they bear inscriptions on their pedestals giving the names of the artists who executed them. The majority of the *madanakai* figures are also represented in miniature in the sixth frieze of the railed parapet.

Beyond the *jagati* or railed parapet we have on the walls around the temple 80 large images, of which only 19 are female. The images are not in a continuous row as in other temples of this style, *e.g.*, the Kēśava temple at Sōmanāthapūr, but stand apart from one another with some interval between them. The figures representing gods and goddesses may be analysed thus:—Vishṇu 32, the same as Lakshmīnārāyaṇa 2, as Vāmana 1, as Narasimha 2, as Varāha 2, as Ranganātha 1, and as Balarāma 1; Śiva and Pārvati, standing, 1; Śiva as the destroyer of Andhakāsura and Gajāsura 3; Harihara 2; Sūrya 4; Pārvati including Durgā and Mahishāsuramardini 5; Bhairava 2; Manmatha and Rati 1; also one each of Gaṇēśa, Brahma, Sarasvati, Garuḍa and Chandra. There are also figures of Rāvaṇa, Daksha, Arjuna, Bali and Śukrāchārya. Two of the large images on the walls, Narasimha in the south-west and Ranganātha in the north-east, are enshrined in ugly structures which mar the beauty of the temple. But from the inscriptions Bēlūr 25 and 30 we learn that these structures were put up in about 1173 and 1588 respectively. There are also figures of gods and goddesses in the third, fifth and sixth friezes of the railed parapet. Four of the large images on the west wall, two representing Vishṇu, one Sarasvati and one Manmatha with Rati, are shown on Plate XVII.

Attached to the outer walls of the *garbha-griha* in the three directions are three elegantly executed car-like niches in two storeys enshrining Vishṇu figures. Each storey is adorned with a railed parapet. On the niches are sculptured from the bottom upwards these friezes—(1) elephants, (2) lions, (3) horsemen, (4) turretted pilasters, and (5) a rail with figures, mostly female, between double columns. Plate XVIII shows the north niche. The outer walls of both the storeys have figures on them. The south niche has on the left outer wall Vishṇu below and Sarasvati above; and on the right wall Vishṇu below and a sixteen-armed Nārāyaṇa seated on a lotus above, a four-armed Garuḍa supporting the lotus with two hands, the other two being folded. The west niche shows on the left wall Vishṇu below and Bhīma attacking Bhagadatta's elephant above; and on the right wall a female figure holding a vessel in the left hand and a flower in the right hand with Garuḍa to the right, below, and Sarasvati and another female figure above. The Vishṇu figure inside is a signed image. The left wall of the north niche shows below a female figure with two children at the sides said to represent Kṛishṇa and Balarāma. The child to the right holds a young lion with a rope. May it represent Bharata, Śakuntalā's son? The upper portion has a female figure. The right wall of the same niche has a female figure below and Durgā above.

A few interesting sculptures in the temple may be noticed here:—Balarāma with a discus in the left hand and a plough in the right; Chandra holding *kumudas* or water-lilies in both the hands; and Narasimha with sixteen hands killing Hiraṇyakaśipu, with Kayādhu, the mother of Prahlāda, and Garuḍa at the sides. The last *madanakai* figure to the left of the north doorway, which represents a huntress, is flanked by two small figures, of which the one to the left is represented as carrying a bamboo lath to the ends of which are tied a deer and a crane shot in the chase; while the other gets a thorn removed from the leg by a seated figure which uses a needle for the purpose. The second *madanakai* figure to the right of the east doorway holds in its hand betel leaves which are true to nature, while the small figure at its left side squirts scented water with a syringe. In the creeper-like canopy of the figure to the left of the north doorway is sculptured on a fruit a fly, perfect in every detail, on which a lizard is preparing to pounce. In the rail or eighth frieze are seen—to the right of the north doorway a king and his queen seated witnessing a wrestling match; also six *Paṇḍārams* or Śaiva devotees with their heads covered; to the left of the same doorway a man with a long coat, hood and *kammarband* or belt in the act of cutting off his head before a seated goddess (perhaps Durgā) who stops him; and to the right of the north-east ugly structure enshrining Ranganātha a chain of destruction—a double-headed eagle or *gaṇḍabhēruṇḍa* attacking a *śarabha*, which attacks a lion, which in its turn attacks an elephant, the latter seizing a snake which is in the act of swallowing a rat—with the figure of a sage wondering at the sight. In the sixth frieze, to the left of the north doorway is observed a female figure stripping itself on finding a lizard in the cloth, the lizard being shown to the left. Similarly, one of the *madanakai* figures, the second figure to the right of the north doorway (Plate VI), is represented as stripping itself on finding a scorpion in the cloth, the scorpion being shown on the base. But people attribute some mysterious power to the figure in the sixth frieze and believe that pouring oil over it wards off the evil effects of a lizard falling on the body. It may be remarked in passing that about sixty-eight figures in this frieze are missing. In the fifth frieze, to the left of the south doorway is seen a female figure drawing a picture on a board; also a figure of the nude Mōhini along with that of Dakshiṇāmūrti dressed in a check long coat with *kammarband*.

In the third frieze are seen two figures carrying a bamboo lath on the shoulders with dead game tied at the ends, figures shooting with guns and a figure of Jina.

At the sides in front of all the three entrances there are two fine pavilions with two more opposite to them at some distance on a lower level, the upper ones containing as a rule figures of Vishṇu and the lower ones those of Bhairava, Mahishâsuramardini and so forth. These pavilions have a frieze of elephants on the base. Plate XIX gives the front view of the upper pavilion to the left of the east entrance and Plate XX a side view of that to the right. There are likewise three more pavilions on a lower level opposite to the three car-like niches around the *garbha-griha*. These have three friezes—elephants, lions and horsemen—on the base. All the nine lower pavilions have figures inside, though in some cases the original figures have been replaced by modern ones. The left lower pavilion at the east entrance has Bhairava and the right, Durgā; the left pavilion at the south entrance has Tāṇḍavēśvara, which is not the original figure, and the right, Brahmāṇi with three faces and the swan emblem; and the left pavilion at the north entrance has Vishṇu, not the original figure, and the right, Mahishâsuramardini. The one opposite to the south car-like niche has Durgā, that opposite to the west niche Vaishṇavi, and that opposite to the north niche Gaṇapati, not the original figure. Each doorway has at the sides the Hoysaḷa crest, *i.e.*, a figure of Saḷa, the progenitor of the Hoysaḷa family, stabbing a tiger. Plate XX shows one of these figures.

The *navaranga* or central hall appears to have been originally left open as in the Kīrti-Nārāyaṇa temple at Talkāḍ[1] without door-frames and screens. In the latter temple the walls subsequently raised conceal the inscriptions on the sides of several of the pillars. The door-frames of the *navaranga* of the Bēlūr temple are surely of a subsequent period as evidenced by the mutilation of the side pillars and the concealment of the inscriptions on them by the figures on the jambs. This fact is borne out by the inscription Bēlūr 72 which tells us that the door-frames, doors and perforated screens were caused to be made by Ballāḷa II (1173-1220), the grandson of Vishṇuvardhana. The *mukha-maṇṭapa* or hall in front of the Kēsava temple, known as the *bali-maṇṭapa*, is a later structure. It is also called Nāgināyaka's

[1] *Mysore Archæological Report* for 1912, para 21.

maṇṭapa owing to a chief of that name having built it. It was in existence before 1557, since Bēlūr 28 records a grant in that year for taking the god to the *maṇṭapa*.

The work inside the Kēśava temple is even finer in some respects than that outside. The image of Kēśava, or Vijaya-Nārāyaṇa as it is named in the inscriptions, is a very handsome figure, about 6 feet high with *prabhā* or halo, standing on a pedestal, about 3 feet high, flanked by consorts. It has four hands, the upper two holding a discus and a conch and the lower two, a lotus and a mace. The *prabhā* has the ten *avatāras* or incarnations of Vishṇu sculptured on it. The *sukhanāsi* doorway, flanked by *dvārapālakas* or doorkeepers, is elegantly executed (Plate XXI). Its pediment, with a figure of Lakshmīnārāyaṇa in the centre, shows excellent filigree work. The *makaras* at the sides bear Varuṇa and his consort on the back. The four pillars in the *sukhanāsi* are later additions. According to Bēlūr 52 they were set up in 1381 to support the dilapidated roof by order of the Vijayanagar king Harihara II by his minister Kampaṇṇa. The beam in front of the *sukhanāsi* doorway has sculptured on it the twenty-four *mūrtis* or forms of Vishṇu. The *navaranga* has raised verandas on both sides of the three entrances. The pillars, which are artistically executed, are of three different sizes, and, with the exception of the central four, all differ from one another in design. The arrangement of the pillars enhances the beauty of the structure. Plate XXII gives the view of a portion of the *navaranga* with its pillars. Two pillars on the verandas at the sides of the east entrance are shown on Plate XXIII. Two other pillars in the *navaranga* deserve special notice. The well-known Narasimha pillar (Plate XXIV), which apparently used formerly to revolve, is carved with minute figures all round from the top to the bottom. One of the figures, a tiny bull, is known as *kaḍale-basava*, because it is of the size of a seed of the Bengal gram (*kaḍale*). A small space on the south face of the pillar is said to have been left blank by the artist who prepared the pillar as a challenge to any artist who can appropriately fill it up. The other pillar, standing to the right of the *sukhanāsi* doorway, shows marvellous filigree work (Plate XXV). It is carved with a female figure in front and has eight vertical bands with fine scroll work the convolutions of which show delicately executed figures representing the Hindu triad of gods, the ten incarnations of Vishṇu, the *ashṭa-dikpālakas* or regents of the eight directions and so forth. There are also lions represented with the faces of other animals. This is perhaps the most beautiful pillar in the temple.

The four central pillars support a large domed ceiling, about 10 feet in diameter and 6 feet deep, which is a grand piece of artistic workmanship remarkable for richness of ornamentation and elaboration of details. Plate XXVI shows a portion of it.[1] The lotus bud depending from the top has Brahma, Vishṇu and Śiva sculptured on it and the bottom frieze illustrates scenes from the Rāmāyaṇa. There are four exquisitely carved female *madanakai* figures standing on the capitals of the four central pillars. Of these, three are signed images. The one on the south-east pillar (Plate XXVII) has a parrot seated on the hand. The bracelet on the hand of this figure can be moved up and down. From the inscription on the pedestal of the image on the south-west pillar (Plate XXVIII) we learn that it represents dancing Sarasvati. The head ornament of this figure can be moved. The figure on the north-east pillar (Plate XXIX) is shown as dressing the hair and the one on the north-west pillar (Plate XXX) as dancing. The remaining ceilings in the *navaranga* are mostly flat and oblong in shape. Those in front of the entrances have the *ashṭa-dikpālakas* sculptured on three separate panels. One of the ceilings at the east entrance has Narasimha killing Hiraṇyakaśipu in the centre (Plate XXXI), the one corresponding to it at the south, Varāha, and that at the north, Kēśava. It will be noticed that these figures are the same as those carved on the pediments of the respective doorways. The ceilings over the verandas show better work than those at the entrances. The west veranda at the south entrance has a frieze depicting scenes from the Rāmāyaṇa.

As stated before, eighteen of the bracket or *madanakai* figures around the temple, three *madanakai* figures in the *navaranga* and the Vishṇu figure in the west car-like niche bear inscribed on their pedestals the names of the artists who prepared them. Such labels have also been noticed in the Kēśava temple at Sōmanāthapūr.[2] Among the names of the artists inscribed in the Kēśava

[1] There is a rafter put across the ceiling for swinging the *utsava-vigraha* or processional image of the temple on certain occasions. As this is not only an eye-sore but also a danger to the safety of the ceiling, it has to be removed and some other arrangement made to swing the god.

[2] *The Kēśava Temple at Sōmanāthapūr*, page 5.

temple at Bēlūr may be mentioned Dāsōja, his son Chāvaṇa, Chikka Hampa, Malliyaṇa, Padari Mallōja, Kencha Malliyaṇṇa, Masada and Nāgōja. It is interesting to note that some of the labels give a few details about the sculptors, such as their native places, parentage, characteristic titles and so forth. Dāsōja and his son Chāvaṇa belonged to Baḷḷigrāme, *i.e.*, Beḷgāmi in the Shikārpūr Taluk of the Shimoga District. The former had the title "smiter of the crowd of titled sculptors" (*biruda-rūvāri-gondaḷa-baḍiva*) and the latter the title "a Śiva to the Cupids titled sculptors" (*biruda rūvāri-Madana-Mahēśa*). Chāvaṇa is also described as a bee at the lotus feet of the god Dharmēśvara of Baḷḷigrāme and is stated to have done his work at the instance of Kēśavadēva. A second title, "a *bhēruṇḍa* to the *śarabhas* rival sculptors" (*machharipa-rūvāri-śarabha-bhēruṇḍa*), is also applied to him. Of Chikka Hampa it is stated that he was Tribhuvanamalla-Dēva's artist, that he prepared some of the images in the *maṇṭapa* or hall of the god Vijaya-Nārāyaṇa built by Hoysaḷa Biṭṭi-Dēva (or Vishṇuvardhana), that he was the son of Inēja and that he had the title "champion over rival sculptors" (*machcharipa-rūvārigaḷa gaṇḍa*). Malliyaṇa calls himself the artist of the mahā-maṇḍalēśvara Tribhuvanamalla capturer of Taḷakāḍu bhujabaḷa-Vīra-Ganga-Hoysaḷa-Dēva (Vishṇuvardhana), and bore the titles "a tiger among sculptors" (*rūvāri-puli*) and "a thunderbolt to the mountains rival titled scluptors" (*machcharipa-biruda-rūvāri-giri-vajradaṇḍa*). It is stated of Padari Mallōja that he was the son-in-law or sister's son (*aḷiya*) of Vadōja of Nālvatubāḍa and had the title "a pair of large scissors to the necks of titled sculptors" (*biruda-rūvāri-gaḷa-gaṇḍagattari*). Nāgōja is described as the artist of the god Svayambhu-Trikūṭēśvara of Gadugu (Gadag), as the delighter of the hearts of the good and as a bee at the lotus feet of Sarasvati. He was the son of Kāṭōja and bore the title "? confounder of sculptors" (*rūvāri-jagadaḷa*). Masada was the son of Yallaṇṇa. Two more labels give some details without naming the artists. One of them styles the artist the Viśvakarma of the Kali age and applies to him the titles "a lion to the elephants titled sculptors" (*biruda-rūvārībha-kaṇṭhīrava*) and "smiter of the crowd of titled sculptors." He belonged to Lokkiguṇḍi. The other label describes the artist as a pupil (*maṇi*) of Tribhuvanamalladēva of the great *agrahāra* (or rent-free village) Bēhūr in the Kuntaḷa country. Another label in which the name of the artist is effaced states that he was the son-in-law or sister's son of Chaḷōja of Nālvatubāḍa and had the title "smiter of the crowd of titled sculptors." This was also the title of Dāsōja, and it is just possible that this and the other label noticed above giving the same title may refer to the same artist.

Four images bear the signature of Dāsōja, four of his son Chāvaṇa, three of Malliyaṇa, two of Chikka Hampa, and one each of Padari Mallōja, Kencha Malliyaṇṇa, Masada and Nāgōja. The two upper figures on Plate XVI, which are also seen on Plate XII, and the figures on Plates XXVIII and XXIX represent four such signed images; the first figure on Plate XVI, which represents a huntress, and the figure on Plate XXIX being the work of Dāsōja, and the second figure on Plate XVI with a monkey pulling at its cloth and the figure on Plate XXVIII, that of his son Chāvaṇa. The figure on Plate XXVII is also a signed image; but the label does not name the artist—it merely states that he was a pupil of Tribhuvanamalladēva of Bēhūr in the Kuntaḷa country. The period of all these sculptors is about 1117, the year in which the god was set up in the temple. There are likewise four more signed images in the buildings outside the Kēśava temple, the names of the sculptors being Bhaṇḍāri Madhuvaṇṇa, Madhuvaṇṇa, Bēchama and Gumma Bīraṇa. It is very probable that these artists belong to a later period. Two of these images, Ādhāra-śakti and Vēṇugōpāla, executed by Bhaṇḍāri Madhuvaṇṇa and Madhuvaṇṇa respectively, are exhibited on Plate XXXII.

A few words may now be said about the other temples and buildings in the enclosure. The Kappe-Chennigarāya temple, situated to the south of the Kēśava temple, measures 124′ by 105′ and has two cells with entrances opposite to each (Plate II). The chief cell with the figure of Kappe-Chennigarāya has a *sukhanāsi* and faces east, while the other with a figure of Vēṇugōpāla faces north. Plate XXXIII gives the east view of the temple. The *sukhanāsi* doorway (Plate XXXIV) is well executed and its pediment, like that of the same doorway in the Kēśava temple, has a figure of Lakshmīnārāyaṇa flanked by *makaras*. Here, however, Varuṇa is represented as seated under a canopy leaning against the *makara* and not as riding it as there. The pediment of the doorway of the other cell has a figure of Narasimha killing Hiraṇyakaśipu flanked on either side by a *makara*, a Vishṇu figure and an elephant. The niches at the sides of the *sukhanāsi* doorway enshrine figures of Lakshmīnārāyaṇa, while those at the sides of the other cell have figures of Sarasvati and Gaṇapati. Opposite to the Sarasvati niche is another with a figure of Mahishâsuramardini (Plate XXXV). The ceilings are elegantly carved. Two of them are shown on Plates XXXVI and XXXVII. The four central pillars of the *navaranga* had once four *madanakai* figures each on their capitals, but now there are only three left. As in the Kēśava temple there are raised verandas on both sides of the entrances. The outer walls have no sculptures. There are three niches in the three directions around the *garbha-griha* of the chief cell. The god Kappe-Chennigarâya is so named because according to tradition there was found in a cavity near the navel of the image a *kappe* or frog. Chennigarâya is a popular name of Chenna-Kēśava or the beautiful Kēśava. The following is the tradition referred to above;—

Kaidāḷa, a village in the Tumkūr Taluk, which formerly bore the name of Krīḍâpura and was the capital of a state, was the native place of the famous architect and sculptor Jakaṇâchâri. His career began while Nṛipa-Râya was ruling in Kṛīḍâpura. He then left his native place and, entering the service of various courts, produced the works by which his fame is to this day upheld. After his departure, a son, Ḍankaṇâchâri, was born to him, who when grown up, set out in search of his father, neither having ever seen the other. At Bēlūr the young man found the Kēśava temple in course of erection and remarked that the image of Chennigarâya had a blemish. As this would be a bar to the image being made an object of worship, the sculptor, who was no other than Jakaṇâchâri himself, hastily vowed to cut off his right hand if any defect could be found in an image he had carved. To test the matter the figure was covered with sandal paste, which dried on every part except around the navel. In this on examination was found a cavity the son had detected, containing a frog and some sand and water. Mortified at the result, Jakaṇâchâri cut off his right hand, and enquiries as to who his critic was, led to the unexpected discovery of their mutual relationship. Subsequently Jakaṇâchâri was directed in a vision to dedicate a temple to the god Kēśava in Krīḍâpura, his native place. Thither he accordingly returned, and no sooner was the temple completed than his right hand was restored. In commemoration of this incident the place has ever since been called *Kaidaḷa*, the restored hand.

On a pillar of the *mahâdvâra* or outer gate of the Kēśava temple at Kaidāḷa is a figure, about 1¼ feet high, standing with folded hands wearing an *uttarīyam* or upper cloth and armed with a dagger, which is said to represent Jakaṇāchāri who built the temple. But this tradition does not appear to be worthy of credence. The existence of a sculptor named Jakaṇāchāri, who is supposed to have built all the artistic structures of different periods in Mysore and elsewhere, is itself doubtful, seeing that no such name has been met with in any of the ornate buildings so far examined, though the names of numerous other sculptors have been noticed. Further, the expression Kaidaḷa does not by any means convey the sense "a restored hand" in Kannaḍa, though both the words *kai* and *taḷa* mean "a hand". Again, the name of the village being Kaidāḷa with a long *a*, the supposed meaning of Kaidaḷa, even if correct, cannot be attached to it. It is very likely that the figure on the pillar, referred to above, represents a chief who caused the temple or the *mahādvāra* to be erected.

An inscription newly discovered on the pedestal of the image of Kappe-Chennigarāya, which consists of an *anushṭubh* verse, states that the image was set up by Śāntale, the seinor queen of Vishṇuvardhana. The incomplete inscription Bēlūr 16 on the wall to the left of the north entrance of the Kappe-Chennigarāya temple, which is similar in contents, as far as it goes, to Bēlūr 58 and 71 recording the consecration of the image of Kēśava (Vijaya-Nārāyaṇa), and which ends with the praises of queen Śāntala-Dēvi, was evidently intended to record the consecration of Kappe-Chennigarāya. Opposite to this temple, near the Elephant's Gate, stands a stone slab carved with a male and a female figure standing side by side with folded hands under an ornamental canopy (Plate XXXVIII). The rich dress and the ornaments with which they are decorated evidently indicate high rank. The male figure wears a cone-shaped cap, partly covering the ears, and a robe extending down to the feet with an *uttarīyam* thrown over it. It also wears large earrings with four? diamonds in each. The female figure is also richly dressed and ornamented. Unfortunately, the faces of the figures are injured, though the other parts are intact. It is highly probable that the figures represent Vishṇuvardhana and his queen Śāntale, who set up respectively the gods Vijaya-Nārāyaṇa and Kappe-Chennigarāya. The Vīra-Nārāyaṇa temple to the west of the Kēśava temple is a small neat building measuring 70′ by 56′. It consists of a *garbha-griha*, a *sukhanāsi* and a *navaranga*, and has a row of large images on the outer walls. Plate XXXIX gives the east view of the temple. The number of large images is 59, of which 36 are female. The deities represented are Vishṇu, Śiva, Brahma, Pārvati, Sarasvati and Bhairava. The sculptures on the north wall representing Bhīma's fight with Bhagadatta and his elephant are very well executed. The west wall shows a peculiar standing figure with three crowned heads. It is richly ornamented and holds a discus and a conch in the upper hands, the other hands being broken. It does not seem to represent Dattātrēya. The inscription Bēlūr 58, of 1117, registers grants for the three gods Vijaya-Nārāyaṇa, Chenna-Kēśava or Chennigarāya and Lakshmīnārāyaṇa. It is probable that the third god is identical with the image in this temple, though it is now known as the Vīra-Nārāyaṇa temple. It will thus be seen that the three temples—the Kēśava, the Kappe-Chennigarāya and the Vīra-Nārāyaṇa—belong to about the same period.

The *garbha-griha*, surmounted by a tower, of the temple of the goddess Sōmanāyaki situated to the south-west of the Kēśava temple is also popularly assigned to the same period (Plate I, left end). The front portion of this temple is said to be a later structure built by a member of the Daḷavāyi family of Kaḷale. The tower of the Kēśava temple, which is no longer in existence, was, it is said, exactly like that of the Sōmanāyaki temple, only much larger in size. According to Fergusson the upper part of the tower was anomalous[1]. But this anomaly can easily be accounted for by the vicissitudes through which the original tower had passed. From Bēlūr 24 we learn that the wood work of the tower having rotted and fallen, it was repaired in 1298 by order of the great minister Khaṇḍeyarāya Sōmeya-daṇṇāyaka. The temple suffered injury at the time of the Muhammadan invasion in 1310, and is said to have been shut up till the time of the Vijayanagar king Harihara II (1377-1404). Bēlūr 63 tells us that in 1387 the tower was repaired and a gold *kalaśa* or finial fixed on it when Muddapa was the minister of Harihara II. According to Bēlūr 64 and 65, the same work was done again in 1736 during the rule of the Mysore king Kṛishṇa-Rāja and the minister Nanja-Rāja, and once again in 1774 when the Mysore king Chāma-Rāja and Navāb Bahadar Haider Ali ruled the earth. With so many vicissitudes it is no wonder that the style of the tower was incongruous. It has been a frequent source of trouble since, and been rebuilt, but has now disappeared altogether.

[1] *History of Indian and Eastern Architecture*, I, 440.

The temple of the goddess Āṇḍāḷ, situated to the north-west of the Kēśava temple, has a row of large images on the outer walls (Plate XL). The basement and the top have also here and there friezes of elephants, scroll work and Purāṇic scenes. The structure has the appearance of having been built with the materials belonging to some ruined temple of an earlier period. The number of large images on the outer walls is 31, of which 19 are female. The canopies over the figures, which differ from one another, show elegant workmanship. Besides the usual deities, Lakshmi and Mōhini are also represented here. Two of the figures on the south wall are signed images executed by Bēchama and Madhuvaṇṇa. The handiwork of Madhuvaṇṇa, which is a figure of Vēṇugōpāla, is shown on Plate XXXII. Plate XLI shows a fine figure of Lakshmīnārāyaṇa flanked by female chauri-bearers on the same wall.

Other temples in the enclosure are those of Jīyar, the Āḻvārs, Narasimha and Rāma, situated in a line to the east of the Kappe-Chennigarāya temple, and those of Dēśikar, Kṛishṇa, Bhāshyakāra or Rāmānujāchārya and Ānjanēya to the east of the Āṇḍāḷ temple. Several of these are later additions. Jīyar, also known as Varavara-muni and Maṇavāḷa-māmuni, was a Śrīvaishṇava teacher and author who flourished in the 14th and 15th centuries. On the south wall of the Jīyar temple is a figure of Ādhāraśakti executed by Bhaṇḍāri Madhuvaṇṇa, which is shown on Plate XXXII. The Āḻvārs are Śrīvaishṇava saints who composed Tamil hymns in praise of Vishṇu known as the *Nālāyira-prabandham* consisting of nearly four thousand stanzas. On the basement of the temple of the Āḻvārs, both inside and outside, runs a frieze representing scenes from the Rāmāyaṇa. Dēśikar, also known as Vēdāntāchārya, was a Śrīvaishṇava teacher and author who lived in the 13th and 14th centuries.

Of the remaining structures in the enclosure, the building in the north-west corner was, according to Bēlūr 20, erected in 1180 by Ballāḷa II to serve as a *koṭṭāra* or granary. We also learn from Bēlūr 2 and 72 that he built the fine pond known as Vāsudēva-sarōvara situated in the north-east corner. At the entrance to this pond are two elephants at the sides, and two pavilions to the north and south. The *manṭapa* to the south of the Vīra-Nārāyaṇa temple is known as the Vāhana-manṭapa, because the temple vehicles (*vāhanas*) are kept there. One of its pillars bears an inscription,

Bēlūr 18, recording a grant in 1292 by the Hoysaḷa king Ballāḷa III, but as the grant relates to a Śiva temple in some other place it is doubtful if the *maṇṭapa* is of this period. The *maṇṭapa* to the south-east of the Kēśava temple, known as the Suvarṇa-maṇṭapa or Kalyāṇa-maṇṭapa, which has a figure of Sugrīva in it, is said to have been built by the Mysore king Kaṇṭhīrava-Narasa-Rāja-Oḍeyar (1638-1659). The building to the south of the north outer gate is the *ugrāṇa* or storehouse and the one adjacent to it, the *pākaśāle* or kitchen. Both have a fine ceiling in front (Plates XLII and XLIII). Bēlūr 72 attributes the erection of the kitchen, as also of the enclosing wall, to Ballāḷa II. Attached to the south of the kitchen is the *yāgaśāle* or the place for offering oblations in the fire, which, according to Bēlūr 13, was built in 1484 by Lakkhaṇṇa-nāyaka, son of Madhuvarasa-nāyaka of Muttagadahāḷu. It is probable that Ballāḷa II who built the enclosing wall (Bēlūr 72) may have also built a *gōpura* or large tower over the north outer gate. At any rate there was a *gōpura* to the temple before 1397, since we learn from Bēlūr 3 that the former *gōpura* having been dismantled and burnt by Ganga-Sālār, the Turuka of Kalburga, the present one was rebuilt with seven storeys in that year by Guṇḍa-daṇḍādhipa, the minister of the Vijayanagar king Harihara II. According to the inscriptions the affairs of the Kēśava temple were managed by a committee of 88 Śrīvaishṇavas. The annual festival of the god Kēśava takes place in April, and it is worthy of note that for three days during the festival the Panchamas have the privilege of entering the courtyard of the temple to pay homage to the god. They also present to the god a pair of large leather sandals once in two or three years. These are kept in the temple and are supposed to be used by the god. When they are worn out, the Panchamas, to whom the fact is revealed in a dream, prepare new ones with great devotion and ceremonial purity and offer them to the god. The other temples in the State which the Panchamas are allowed to enter during the annual festival are the Nārāyaṇasvāmi temple at Mēlkōṭe in the Seringapatam Taluk and the Ranganāthasvāmi temple on the Biḷigirirangan Hills in the Yeḷandūr Taluk. They likewise present sandals to the gods in these places.

We may now proceed to say a few words about the inscriptions relating to the temple. Several of them have already been briefly referred to. The most important of these epigraphs is Bēlūr 58, which records the consecration of the temple in 1117 by Vishṇuvardhana (Plate XLIV.) It is a long inscription of 85 lines consisting of Sanskrit and Kannaḍa stanzas and Kannaḍa prose passages which are almost wholly made up of Sanskrit words. After an invocatory verse in praise of Kēśava and Śiva, the epigraph proceeds to give the usual account of the rise of the Yadu race and the Hoysaḷas and their genealogy down to Vishṇuvardhana who is praised at considerable length. Of Vinayāditya it is stated [1] that when he set forth for war the Konkaṇigas, saying "the water of his sword will drown us," scattered pell-mell in every direction and that the hill chiefs, dreading his valour, came and placed their heads at his lotus feet. His queen was Keḷeyabbe. Their son was Eṟeganga. The celebrated Dhārā, the chief city of the valiant Māḷava kings, which Bhōja by victory over hostile kings had enlarged, he took as if the preliminary sip (*āpōśana*) before feasting on the dominions of his enemies. He also burnt Bhōja's principal fortresses. The burning of Baḷeya-paṭṭaṇa on the sea-shore by the flames of Eṟeganga's anger, recalled to mind the appearance of the waves of the sea when consumed by Rāma's fiery arrow. His queen was Ēchala-Dēvi. They had three sons—Ballāḷa, Vishṇu and Udayāditya. Breaking with their swords the pride of Pāṇḍya, who opposed them with arrogance, Vishṇu and Ballāḷa seized the goddess of his sovereignty. In Dōrasamudra they defeated the army of Jagadēva and captured his treasury. His god being Mahēśa, his wife the goddess of Victory, the group of his dependants the whole earth, his relations by marriage his equals—the world-renowned Ballāḷa was truly great.

Victorious is Vishṇu-Dēva, enjoyer of learned discourses in the assembly of clever scholars, a student of the Bharata-śāstra, a favorite of the goddess of Victory and a constant worshipper of Purushōttama. First taking into his arms the goddess of the Poysaḷa kingdom, he brought all the points of the compass under his command, and capturing Taḷakāḍu, became the first to the Ganga kingdom. He burnt the chief city of the Gangas. In order that Rājēndra-Chōḷa, disgusted at the water of the Kāvēri suddenly becoming polluted, should be driven to the use of water from wells in the vicinity, Vishṇu by the power of his arm made the hostile army drown in the stream of the river, and caused his own valour to shine forth. Then follow long

[1] In what follows only important facts are noticed, mere laudations being omitted.

strings of epithets applied to Vishṇuvardhana, his queen Śāntala-Dēvi, the Kēśava temple and the god Kēśava.

When the mahā-maṇḍalēśvara who has acquired the band of five great instruments, lord of the excellent city of Dvārāvati, the foundation pillar of the palace kingly *dharma* adorned with the finial the Yadu race, obtainer of boons from Vāsantikādēvi, delighter in bowing to the lotus feet of Mukunda, (and with numerous other epithets, among which are), proficient in the art of poetry music logic grammar the Vēdas and the Purāṇas, lord of Gaṇḍagiri, an untimely thunderbolt in splitting the rock Pāṇḍya, terrifier of the Tuḷu king, a Bhairava in destroying the army of Jagaddēva, a lion to the elephant Sōmeśvara, displayer of his valour before Māṇikyadēvi of the Chakrakūṭa throne, destroyer of the pride of Adiyama, a gale in overturning the tree Narasimhabrahma, gratifier of the *yōginis* or female spirits with draughts of blood out of the skull-cup of Kaḷapāḷa, a Garuḍa to the serpent Chengiri, king of the hill chiefs, a fierce elephant in destroying the garden Irungōḷa, a Vainya in shaking with his bow the mountain Chengiri Permāḷa, establisher with his army of Paṭṭi-Permāḷa, capturer of Taḷavanapura (Talkāḍ) the Kongu country Noḷambavāḍi Nīla-parvata and Kōḷāḷapura, attacker of Kovatūr Teriyūr Vallūr Nangalipura Ghaṭṭakapāṭa and Kānchīpura, builder of the wonderful Vijaya-Nārāyaṇa temple with the wealth acquired by the strength of his arm, bearer of the tiger crest, lord of Vēda-parvata sanctified by the penance of Brahma, champion over the Malapas, a swan sporting in the gardens on the banks of the Kāvēri, a victorious Nārāyaṇa, the illustrious Tribhuvanamalla-bhujabaḷa-Vīra-Ganga-Vishṇuvardhana-Poysaḷa-Dēva was protecting by the power of his arm a dominion bounded on the east by Nangali, on the south by Kongu Chēram and Anamale, on the west by Bārakanūr in Konkaṇa, and on the north by Sāvimale—

And when, in company with the senior queen (with many epithets, among which are), a Kamale born in the milk-ocean of Balipura, obtainer of boons from the god Dharmēśvara, builder of the Rāmeśvara temple at Īśapura, a moon in increasing the volume of the ocean of affection in the heart of Vishṇuvardhana, rejoicer in bowing to the lotus feet of Pārvati, proficient in all arts, an earnest student of the Bharatāgama, a crest-jewel in dancing, a jewel of protection to all faiths, a Sarasvati in singing, a rutting elephant to co-wives, the crowned consort Śāntala-Dēvi,——Vishṇuvardhana-Poysaḷa-Dēva was in his residence in the great city of Vēlāpura, ruling the kingdom in peace and wisdom—

He set up with great devotion in a fine lofty temple, which was characterised by all the marks of auspiciousness and adorned with female stone figures, rows of lions and elephants, towers and banners, (with many more epithets conveying a double meaning), the god Vijaya-Nārāyaṇa (described with a number of epithets), and, on Vaḍḍavāra the fifth lunar day of the bright fortnight of Chaitra in the year Hēmaḷambi corresponding to the Śaka year 1039, in order to provide for the daily and occasional enjoyments and the offerings at the three times of the gods Vijaya-Nārāyaṇa, Chenna-Kēśava and Lakshmī-Nārāyaṇa, and for the livelihood of the temple servants (specified), granted a number of villages (named). It was ordered by the eleventh incarnation, Vishṇuvardhana-Hoysaḷa-Dēva, that the surplus after meeting the expenditure and the income from devotees should be devoted to temple repairs.

Of the remaining inscriptions relating to the temple, the one on the pedestal of Vijaya-Nārāyaṇa or Kēśava states that the victorious king Vishṇu, protector of the whole earth, caused to be made the image of Vijaya- Nārāyaṇa, the god of gods; while the one on the pedestal of Kappe-Chennigarāya tells us that the setting up of the god Chenna-Kēśava, bringing peace to all the creatures of the world, was carried out by Śāntala-Dēvi, the queen and crowned consort of Vishṇu. Two records, Bēlūr 15 and 25, refer themselves to the reign of Nārasimha I, son of Vishṇuvardhana. The former, which is mostly defaced, seems to register a grant for the god Vijaya-Nārāyaṇa. The latter, dated 1173, records a grant of land by the *mahā-pasāyita* (master of the robes) Śrīvaishṇava-Tirumale to provide for offerings of rice for the god Narasimha enshrined in the ugly structure attached to the outer wall of the Kēśava temple in the south-west, and for food to the Śrīvaishṇavas from other places. Of the reign of Ballāḷa II, son of Nārasimha I, there are four inscriptions—Bēlūr 2, 20, 59 and 72. Of these, Bēlūr 59, which appears to be the earliest, being dated in 1174, states that the king remitted all the petty taxes in the twelve villages and their hamlets belonging to the god Vijaya-Nārāyaṇa, and that, for the performance of prayers, sacrifices, daily service and recitations of the Vēdas in the Kēśava temple, he granted certain villages (named) to the 120 *bhaṭṭas* of

Kēśavapura, the 21 of Śubhapura and the 30 Śrīvaishṇava *sthānikas* of Bēlūr. He also gave a village for the supply of milk to the god. Bēlūr 20, dated 1180, records that he erected a *koṭṭāra* or granary for the temple, giving it the name of Yakshēśa-bhaṇḍāra, and Bēlūr 2 tells us that he had a pond made for the god Vijaya-Nārāyaṇa and named it the Vāsudēva-sarōvara. Lastly, Bēlūr 72 informs us that he caused to be made of stone for Vijaya-Nārāyaṇa pierced windows, secure door-frames, kitchen, granary, ramparts and the Vāsudēva pond. It also refers to his capture of the fortress of Uchchangi. There is only one record of the reign of Nārasimha III, son of Sōmēśvara, namely, Bēlūr 73, which registers the grant of the village Bikkigōḍu for the god Chenna-Kēśava of Bēlūr. Ten epigraphs, most of which are dated 1298, fall into the reign of Ballāḷa III, though he is not named in them. Of these, Bēlūr 24 says that by order of the great minister Sōmeya-daṇṇāyaka the wood work in the tower of the Kēśava temple, which had rotted, broken and fallen, was strengthened and all the fallen bricks restored by the officer Rangaṇṇa, and Bēlūr 66 tells us that the same minister, in order to provide for plantains, garlands and certain festivals (specified) for the god Kēśava, and for the feeding of ascetics and pilgrims, had funds deposited with the Śrīvaishṇavas of the temple with the condition that all these works of merit should be carried on from the accrued interest, and caused these grants to be inscribed on the west wall of the south entrance. The wall referred to has engraved on it eight inscriptions giving details of the grants and the expenditure to be incurred in connection with the several items.

There are nearly twenty records belonging to the Vijayanagar period. Five of them, namely, Bēlūr 3, 52, 61, 62 and 63, refer themselves to the reign of Harihara II. The earliest of these, Bēlūr 52, dated 1381, states that by order of the king the great minister Kampaṇṇa repaired the dilapidated roof of the *sukhanāsi* of the Kēśava temple by setting up four pillars as props. Bēlūr 63 tells us that, during the time of the minister Muddapa, Malagarasa of the famous Kāśmīra family adorned the Kēśava temple with a golden *kalaśa* or finial in 1387. Bēlūr 61 and 62, found on two lamp-stands of bell-metal, state that the lamp-stands were presented to the temple in 1395 by Guṇḍapa-daṇṇāyaka, the house minister of the king. The men who prepared them were Kāḷōja and Anakōja, sons of the brazier

Mārāḷa-Mindōja of Paṭaṇa. The fifth inscription, Bēlūr 3, which appears to be dated 1397, opens with a number of verses in praise of the god Kēśava and after giving briefly the pedigree of Harihara II goes on to give a long account of the valour and exploits of his minister Guṇḍa-daṇḍādhipa. We are then told that by order of the king this minister restored the grants which Vishṇuvardhana had made for the god Kēśava, his family deity, and which had by lapse of time been greatly reduced; laid down rules for the performance of all the services (67 specified) formerly ordained by Vishṇuvardhana; and rebuilding with seven storeys the *gōpura* or great tower over the outer gate, which Ganga-Sālār, the Turuka of Kallubarage, had dismantled and burnt, set up on its summit a golden *kalaśa*. Then follow several verses in praise of the *gōpura*. Bēlūr 56, an inscription referring itself to the reign of Bukka II, records the gift in 1405 of a white conch-shell ornamented with gold for the god Kēśava by the king's house minister Heggappa and Mallarasa. Bēlūr 14, an inscription of the time of Dēva-Rāya I, dated 1414, records that his great minister Baiche-daṇṇāyaka caused to be erected a lamp-pillar (see Plate I) for the Kṛittikā festival of lights and a swing for the swinging festival of the god Kēśava. Three records, Bēlūr 11, 13 and 70, all dated in 1484, relate to a chief named Lakkhaṇṇa-nāyaka, who was the son of Madhuvarasa-nāyaka of Muttagadahāḷu. Bēlūr 13 records the erection of the *yāgaśāle* in the Kēśava temple and the other two, grants by him to provide for certain festivals of the god. There are two epigraphs, Bēlūr 57 and 78, of the reign of Kṛishṇa-Dēva-Rāya. The former, dated 1518, registers a grant for the god by Singappa-nāyaka for the merit of the king; while the latter, dated 1524, records that Basavappa-Nāyaka, a servant of the king, constructed a pond for the floating festival of the god Kēśava, the family deity of the king, and a Vasanta-maṇṭapa, for the spiritual welfare of his parents, and made a grant of two villages (named) to provide for the expenses of the festival. Bēlūr 4, dated 1548, tells us that during the rule of Sadāśiva-Rāya Chikka-Singapa-Nāyaka granted a village to provide for the car festival of the god Kēśava, the family deity of the king. Bēlūr 1 and 12 are records of the reign of Śrī-Ranga-Rāya I: the former, dated 1578, tells us that....yana-rāja granted a village to provide for the daily offerings and those on the monthly and yearly birthdays of Rāmānujāchārya, the servant of the feet of the god Kēśava, in order that merit might accrue to the king, Venkaṭādri-Nāyaka and his own parents; while the latter, dated 1580, records the erection of a *maṇṭapa* of 15 *ankaṇas* near the Elephant's Gate for swinging the god Kēśava during the spring festival by the Bēlūr chief Venkaṭādri-Nāyaka, son of Eṟa-Kṛishṇapa-Nāyaka. From Bēlūr 7, of 1566, we learn that the same chief built the Garuḍa shrine in front of Nāgināyaka's maṇṭapa.

Of the records that remain to be noticed, Bēlūr 23, dated 1579, states that the stone cot kept in the Kalyāṇa-maṇṭapa was presented to the temple by Honnājiyamma, daughter of Raghunāthaya and Peddājiyamma; Bēlūr 30, dated 1588, records the erection of the structure enshrining Ranganātha, attached to the outer wall of the Kēśava temple in the north-east, by Tiruvengaḷaya for the spiritual welfare of Raghunāthaya and his consort Peddamma; Bēlūr 22, of 1626, records the construction of a veranda of 26 *ankaṇas* in the north of the temple enclosure by Mūrtiyappa-Nāyaka and Puṭṭaṇṇa-Nāyaka, servants of Kṛishṇappa-Nāyaka's son Venkaṭādri-Nāyaka, in order that merit might accrue to their parents; and Bēlūr 8, dated 1696, tells us that Kēśava-rāya, son of Chenniga-rāya, caused the *balipīṭha* (or stone pedestal on which the oblations are offered) in Nāgi-nāyaka's maṇṭapa to be erected according to the rules of the Pancharātra. Three inscriptions relate to the kings of Mysore. One of them, Bēlūr 29, dated 1717, refers itself to the reign of Kṛishṇa-Rāja-Oḍeyar I and records the construction of a pond and a *maṇṭapa* in front of the temple for the spring water-festival of the god by Kappayya, son of Nanjappayya, and a money grant by him for the expenses of the festival; another, Bēlūr 64, of 1736, states that during the rule of Kṛishṇa-Rāja (II) and the minister Nanja-Rāja a chief named Venkaṭa had a *kalaśa* fixed on the tower of the Kēśava temple; and the third, Bēlūr 65, dated 1774, tells us that the same work was done once again by Nanjayārya during the rule of Chāma-Rāja (VIII) and Navāb Bahadar Haidar Ali. We may also notice here the inscriptions on some of the temple jewels and vessels. A gold hand belonging to the temple of the goddess bears an inscription stating that it was presented by the Mysore king Kṛishṇa-Rāja-Oḍeyar I in 1713. From the inscriptions on a silver pitcher and a gold cup in the temple we learn that they were presents from Rangaiya of Aigūr, a servant of Kṛishṇa-Rāja-Oḍeyar

III of Mysore, in 1829 and 1830 respectively. A gold necklace set with precious stones was, as indicated by the inscription on it, a gift from Nanjammaṇṇi, wife of Kṛishṇe-arasu, in about 1840.

Some of the inscriptions noticed above and extracts from some of the longer ones are given in the Appendix at the end.

At a short distance to the west of Bēlūr is situated the Śankarēśvara temple (Plate XLV), a Hoysaḷa structure, consisting of a *garbha-griha* or adytum, a *sukhanāsi* or vestibule and a Nandi-manṭapa. The *navaranga* or middle hall is gone, only the base being left. The *garbha-griha* is surmounted by a stone tower. The *sukhanāsi* doorway is well executed. It has perforated screens at the sides and a well carved pediment with Tāṇḍavēśvara in the centre flanked by *makaras*. The *garbha-griha* and *sukhanāsi* have flat ceilings carved with lotuses. There is also a good figure of Tāṇḍavēśvara in front of the embankment over the *sukhanāsi*. The outer walls have single and double pilasters surmounted by miniature turrets. To the north of the temple is a small plain shrine of the goddess.

Fergusson makes the following remarks[1] in connection with the Bēlūr temple :—

"There are many buildings in India which are unsurpassed for delicacy of detail by any in the world, but the temples of Belur and Halebid surpass even these for freedom of handling and richness of fancy.

Belur temple.—The character of the design of the base under the windows is perhaps as perfect an example of the decorative skill of a Hindu architect as any to be found in India. The main lines are everywhere carried through without interruption, while the variety and elegance of the pattern is only such as could issue from the fertile brain, or be executed by the patient hands, of a Hindu artist. It (the temple) combines constructive propriety with exuberant decoration to an extent not often surpassed in any part of the world.

Andal shrine.—Its ornaments are sculptures taken from some earlier temple which has been ruined. These sculptures are as perfect as any to be found in this neighbourhood. Not only are the figures themselves elegant and freer from exaggeration than is generally found even in this district,

---

[1] *Architecture in Dharwar and Mysore*, 44, 48, and 49.

but the canopies over them are characterised by singular elegance of detail and beauty of design".

In his *History of Indian and Eastern Architecture*[1], which contains a woodcut of one of the perforated screens of the Bēlūr temple, he says:—

"It is not, however, either to its dimensions, or the disposition of its plan, that this temple owes its pre-eminence among others of its class, but to the marvellous elaboration and beauty of its details. The following woodcut will convey some idea of the richness and variety of pattern displayed in the windows of the porch. The pierced slabs themselves, however, are hardly so remarkable as the richly carved base on which they rest, and the deep cornice which overshadows and protects them. The amount of labour, indeed, which each facet of this porch displays is such as, I believe, never was bestowed on any surface of equal extent in any building in the world; and though the design is not of the highest order of art, it is elegant and appropriate, and never offends against good taste.

The sculptures of the base of the vimana are as elaborate as those of the porch, in some places more so. The upper part of the tower is anomalous. It may be that it has been repaired till it has assumed its present discordant appearance."

In Workman's *Through Town and Jungle* (page 85), which contains a few views of the same temple, these remarks occur:—

"The Belur temple stands in a court which is entered through a profusely decorated gopura. It has several pavilions, but the chief attraction is the large and elegant porch with stone windows cut like those at Somanathpur in many patterns but more elaborate. These windows are extremely ornamental and perfectly adapted to this style of architecture".

[1] I, 439-440.

APPENDIX.

Inscriptions relating to the Kesava Temple at Belur.

Belur, 58. 1117. (Extracts).

श्रीमत्त्रैलोक्यपूज्याय सर्वकर्मसुसाक्षिणे ।
फलदाय नमो नित्यं केशवाय शिवाय च ॥
श्रीशोदराम्बुजभवादुदितोऽत्रिरत्रिजातेन्दुपुत्रबुधपुत्रपुरूरवस्तः ।
आयुस्ततश्च नहुषो नहुषाद्ययातिस्तस्माच्च यदुर्यदुकुले बहवो बभूवुः ॥
ख्यातेषु तेषु नृपतिः कथितः कदाचित्
कश्चिद्वने मुनिवरेण सळः करालम् ।
शार्दूलकं प्रति हि पोय् सळ इत्यतोऽभूत्
तस्याभिधा मुनिवचोऽपि चमूरुलक्ष्म ॥
ततो द्वारावतीनाथाः पोय्सळा द्वीपिलाञ्छनाः ।
जाताः शशपुरे तेषु विनयादित्यभूपतिः ॥
मण्डलाग्रसमुत्पन्नतेजसा द्विड्बलाब्धयः ।
आकृष्य जीवनं तेन निःशेषं शोषिता भुवि ॥
प्रीतिं स स्वकरेण विश्वभुवनस्योत्पादयन् चन्द्रवत्
भीतिं वैरिकुलेषु दण्डमुखतः सम्पादयन् धर्मवत् ।
स्फीतिं साधुजने निजावतरणादारोपयन् कृष्णवत्
चक्रे शुक्लतरं वरो निजयशश्चक्रेण चक्रं भुवः ॥
स श्रीवृद्धिकरं करं जनहितं कृत्वा धरां पालयन्
श्वेतच्छत्रसहस्रपत्रकमले लक्ष्मीं चिरं वासयन् ।
दोर्दण्डे रिपुखण्डनैकचतुरे वीरश्रियं नाटयन्
चिक्षेपाखिलदिक्षु शिक्षितरिपुस्तेजः प्रशस्तोदयः ॥
कोंकणिगरिवन खड्ग्द । कंकणवदे नम्मनेलवो मुळुगिसुगेनुतुं ॥
भोंकल् केदरुविनं नि । शशंकं परियिट्टनल्ते विनयादित्यं ॥

मलेयरसुमकळेल्लं। तलेयं तडवुत्तमेळ्दु पादांबुजमं ॥
तलेयोळ् तळेवेनेगं भुज। बलमं तळेदिर्पनल्ते विनयादित्यं ॥
लेखेव वेलेव सुमेखलेव सुधांशुबिम्बस्य सुधाम्बुराशेः।
सुराचलस्याभवदग्रभामा तस्य प्रिया श्रीकेळेयब्बनामा ॥
गङ्गापयोध्योरिव पुण्यहेतुः सङ्गस्तयोरप्यभवत्सुहेतुः।
पुत्रस्ततोभूदेरगङ्गनामा सीमा गुणग्रामभृतां प्रसिद्धः ॥
कृपया च कृपाणेन प्रजा भूमेश्च कण्टकान्।
रक्षन् धर्मसुतो जातः क्षत्रधर्मसुताप्रियः ॥
स श्रीवल्लभपादपल्लवलुठच्चेतःप्रसूनस्सदा
वक्षःश्रीनयनप्रभाधवलिते दोर्दण्डवज्रालये।
बिभ्राणो धरणीं ककुब्जयभरप्रस्फारभेरीरवाद्
गोत्रोर्वीधरसुप्तसिंहहृदयस्फोटं चकार स्फुटम् ॥
धाराधारो भुजबलवतां मालवाधीश्वराणां
भोजेनौजोविजितरिपुणा वर्द्धिता या प्रसिद्धा।
साभूदापोशनमहितभूभोजने यस्य पूर्व
कौबेराशाविजयसमये वर्ण्यते किं स वीरः ॥
पोगेपोक्काशाधिपर्कण्गळनोरसुविनं दिग्गजापांडुदंतं।
पोगेसुत्तल्कर्गिकोडिर्पिनमपवनमागिर्दं रोदोंतरालं ॥
पोगेयिंदं मेघवृन्दान्वितमेनिसुविनं तीव्रतेजोनलं कै।
मिगुवंनं पोय्सळं भोजन कुरुपिन दुर्गगळं कूडे सुट्टं ॥
करेविडिदु बळेयवट्टण। मुरिवुदुवेरेगंगनृपन कोपानलर्गं ॥
स्मरियिसिदुदु रामशर। स्पुरिताप्रियनब्धिवीचिनिचयाचकितं ॥
आनरपतिगंभोधिग। नूनगभीरतेये समनिसिर्पतिरे स ॥
न्मानिनियेचलदेवि म। नोनयनप्रीति समनिसल् समनिसिदळ्
उभयकुलशुद्धेयेनिपा। शुभलक्षणेगं सुचरितचरितनेनिप्पा ॥
प्रभुगं मूवर्तनयर्। सुभगर् बल्लाळविष्णुवुदयादित्यर् ॥
मददिनिदिराद पांड्यन। मदमं निजखड्गजलदे कर्चिये कळेदो ॥
वदे राज्यलक्ष्मियं को। ळ्ळदटर् केवलमे विष्णुबल्लाळनृपर् ॥
दोरसमुद्रदल्लि जगदेवन सेनेयनिक्कि तम्म तोळ्।

वीरसमुद्रमागे जयलक्ष्मिगे तद्भुजवक्त्ररक्षका ॥
ङ्गारविलेपमं नेरपि तत्पदकंबरसेय्दे कोडु भं ।
डारमनानृपर् तळेद वीरमनारो गभीरमेन्नदर् ॥
परमाराध्यं महेशं कुलवधु विजयश्री नेलं पोष्यवर्ग ।
दोरेगळ् वैवाहसंबंधिगळेने नेगळ्दारायरंभोजजांडो ॥
दरदोळ् तेंगायनीरंतिरे तिळिदजसं तन्न भंडारमागु ।
त्तिरे बल्लाळावनीशं पोगळे जगमशेषं महत्वक्के नोंतं ॥
जयति धरणिलोकोत्तंसितात्मीयपादः चतुरविबुधगोष्ठीप्रौढवाणीविनोदः ।
सकलभरतविद्याहृद्यगम्भीरभावः विपुलविजयलक्ष्मीवल्लभो विष्णुदेवः ॥
निगूढमन्त्राङ्घ्रिपदो बलान्वितः स्वभावशौण्डीरकठोरकर्परः ।
बिभर्ति भूभारमतुच्छकच्छपः तदीयबाहुर्घनखड्गकन्धरः ॥
यदध्वरावुद्धतधूमसञ्चयात् घनीभवन्मेघचये चरन् गजः ।
शतक्रतोः कार्ष्ण्यमुपेत्य जायते भयाय धन्यो नृपतिः स भूतले ॥
सदा नियोगः पुरुषोत्तमार्चने धरावने दानचये फलप्रदे ।
करस्य चित्रं नृपतेः सकर्मणः कठोरमार्गों मृदुता च दृश्यते ॥
भूसीमाचलचक्रपूर्णयशसा सम्पूर्णबिम्बोदयः
विष्णुः खेचरमिन्दुमेणतिलकं शार्दूलसल्लाञ्छनः ।
तेजस्तीव्रतरोऽप्यपूर्वहिमकृत्पूर्वं हसन् सर्वदा
एकस्थानशिखामणि विजयते लोकैकचूडामणिः ॥
नीतिर्यत्प्रातिहार्ये चरति नियमतः काल एव स्वकृत्ये
धृत्वा यत्खड्गमुग्रं क्षणमपि न चला वर्त्तते वीरलक्ष्मीः ।
यस्य श्वेतातपत्रच्छाविपिहितवपुर्भूर्भुजे स्वस्थमास्ते
स श्रीमान् पादपीठीकृतरिपुमकुटो भासते विष्णुदेवः ॥
विष्णौ पश्चिमदिग्जयप्रचलितं किं वर्ण्यते तद्बलं
पीते यद्रजसा रिपुं मृगपतेवामग्नमब्धेर्जले ।
निःशेषं मुखशोषमेत्य बडवाग्नौ निष्प्रभे सप्रभं
दातुं रत्नमुपायनं जलाधिपो दृष्टो हठाद्विष्णवे ॥
मोदलोळ् पोय्सळराज्यलक्ष्मियोदवं तोळ्वलिपिनिं ताळ्दि त ।
न्नुदयं रंजिसे तन्न बल्पोदवे तन्नापेरे तन्नाके मी ॥

रे दिशाचक्रमनोत्तिकोंडु तलकाडं गङ्गराज्यके तां।
मोदलादं यदुवंशवर्धनकरं श्रीविष्णुभूपालकं॥
पिंगदे तोळोळ् कोर्वि म। लंगिरं जयलक्ष्मि लक्ष्मि वर्धिसे सुट्टं॥
गंगर कुरुपिन पुरमं। तुंगबलं विष्णुवेंब भुजबलगंगं॥
पले कावेरिय वारि कूडे पोलसादत्तेंदु पेवग्सुतुं।
केलदोळ् कूपजलासियप्पिनेगमाराजेंद्रचोळं भुजा॥
बलदिं विष्णु तदीयसेनेय पेणंगळ् तन्नदीपूरदोळ्।
कलसल् विक्रमकेळियं मेरेदनत्युग्रप्रतापोदयं॥

स्वस्तिसमधिगतपञ्चमहाशब्द महामण्डलेश्वरनुं, द्वारावतीपुरवरेश्वरनुं, यदुकुलकलश-कलितनृपधर्महर्म्यमूलस्तम्भनुं, अप्रतिहतप्रतापविदितविजयारम्भनुं, वासन्तिकादेवीलब्धवरप्रसादनुं, श्रीमन्मुकुन्दपादारविन्दवन्दनविनोदनुं, अक्षुण्णलक्ष्मीलक्षितवक्षःप्रदेशनुं, प्रतिदिनोपचीयमानपुण्यप्रवेशनुं, विनमदहितभयचकितमुखविम्बावळम्बस्फटिकपादपीठविन्यस्तपदतलनुं-श्वेतातपत्रशीतळीकृतभूतळनुं, स्नेहनिहितराजलक्ष्मीकटाक्षच्छटायमानधवळचमररुहोपवीज्यमाननुं, शौण्डीरसरसवीरकथाकर्णनोत्तीर्णहर्षपुलकसन्ताननुं, रिपुविजयविदिताविविधरत्नखचितकर्णकुण्डलप्रभामण्डलस्थगितगण्डमण्डलनुं, अनूनविभवालोकनागमनोत्कण्ठिताखण्डलनुं, विकटवक्षःस्थलविराजमानविपुलविमलमुक्ताफलविकीर्णकान्तिदन्तुरितकेयूरकीर्तिमुखनुं, मृदुमधुरवचनमिलितमन्दस्मितसुधारसस्यन्दिवदनविधुबिम्बप्रसादसखनुं, बहुसमरलब्धविजयारूढविक्रमातिकर्कशभुजयुगलनुं, भटकटकभुजाटनोत्कण्ठविजयलक्ष्मीदृढोकरण निहितखड्गनिगलनुं, सेवागमनसमयसमदकामिनीकदम्बचलनचलाशिञ्जिनीसञ्जातमञ्जुनादोद्बुद्धकुसुमबलिशबलमधुकरनिकरझङ्कारमुखरितास्थानरङ्गनुं, नीतिनितम्बिनीहृदयनिहितगभीरान्तरङ्गनुं, वीरलक्ष्मीविहारसफलशखनन्दनाभिरामनुं, शरणागतकुभृत्कुलनियुक्तक्षेमनुं, सङ्गीतप्रसङ्गभङ्गिसङ्गतचतुरभरतनुं, तर्कविद्याविशारदविचारनिरतनुं, शब्दविद्यासमग्रलक्षणसुशिक्षनुं, वेदविद्यापरीक्षादक्षनुं, सकलपुराणपुञ्जितार्थरत्नकोशनुं, पुरुषार्थसार्थमूलसत्यमणिभूषनुं, कवित्वतत्वनिशितबुद्धियुं, अवन्ध्यमन्त्रसिद्धियुं, लोकालोकनश्रीकराकारनुं, सत्त्वसमुत्पन्नशोभादिगुणाधारनुं, काम्भोजवाजिराजिसञ्चरणतरलधरणीवलयनुं, विजयकदलिकाकदम्बचुम्बितावियद्वलयनुं, गजराजगण्डविजयडिण्डिमायमानोद्भमरमधुकरपटलघटितपिञ्छातपत्रनुं, परवधूपुत्रनुं, करालकरवालशार्दूलनिर्धूतमण्डलिकमृगयूथनुं, गण्डगिरिनाथनुं, पाण्ड्यगण्डशैलनिर्भेदनाकालदम्भोलियुं, तुळुनृपालहृदयविदलनप्रकटरणकेळियु, जगदेवबलविलयभैरवनुं, सोमे-

श्वरप्रचण्डवेतण्डकबलनप्रबलकण्ठीरवनुं, चक्रकूटपीठमाणिक्यदेवीसमक्षलक्षसमराटोपनुं, अदियमावलेपलोपनिपुणचापनुं, नरसिंहब्रह्मभूजभञ्जनप्रभञ्जननुं, कळपालकपालचषकशोणितापानतुष्टयोगिनीमनोरञ्जननुं, चेङ्गिरिभुजङ्गभङ्गकरखड्गखगराजनुं, मलराजराजनुं, इरुङ्गोलकुन्तकदलवनविदलनकरालशुण्डालनुं, बलपदोद्धूतधूलीधूसरितदिक्पालनुं, चेङ्गिरिपेर्माळकुत्कीलचालनचतुरचापवैन्यनुं, पट्टिपेर्माळप्रतिष्ठानुष्ठितात्मसैन्यनुं, आत्मीकृततळवनपुरनुं, अङ्गीकृतकोङ्गविषयनुं, अवलम्बितनोळम्बवाडियुं, दूरीकृतारिवर्गनुं, ऊरीकृतनीलपर्वतनुं, उररीकृतकोळालपुरनुं, उन्मूलितकोवतूरनुं, उत्तरलिततेरियूरनुं, उल्लङ्घितवल्लूरनुं, उद्घाटितनङ्गलिपुरनुं, उत्पाटितघट्टकपाटनुं, उत्कम्पितकाञ्चीपुरनुं, उद्दण्डितप्रचण्डतेजनुं, उत्तम्भितकीर्तिध्वजनुं, उज्जृम्भितविजयभेरीरवनुं, भुजबलावष्टम्भसम्भूतवित्तविरचितविचित्रविजयनारायणोत्तुङ्गभवननुं, वीरवितरणविलासकुलाभिमानिनुतिमुखरसकलभुवननुं, कायकान्तिपरिहसितकाञ्चननुं, शार्दूललाञ्छननुं, पञ्चसप्ततपःपूतवेदपर्वताधीश्वरनुं, राजसमाजभास्वरनुं, यशःप्रसरपरिपूर्णपद्मजाण्डनुं, मलपरोळ्गण्डनुं, कावेरीतीरवनविहारमदमरालनुं, सुभटसमरकेलिलोलनुं, लोकोपकारपरायणनुं, विजयनारायणनुं, आळि मुनिरिवनुं, शौर्यमं मेरेवनुं, एनिसिद श्रीमत्त्रिभुवनमल्ल भुजबलवीरगङ्ग विष्णुवर्धन पोय्सळदेवर्, मूडल् नङ्गलिय पडिय घट्टम, तेङ्कल् कोङ्गु चेरमनमले, पडुवल् कोङ्कणद बारकनूरघट्टवादियागि, बडगल् साविमलेयिंदोळगाद भूमियं भुजबलावष्टम्भदिं परिपालिसुत्तं ॥

स्वस्तिसमस्तमङ्गलाभ्युदयकरलक्षणाभिरामेयुं, सौभाग्यसीमेयुं, बलिपुरवरक्षीरवाराशिजनितकमलेयुं, विशुद्धाचारविमलेयुं, श्रीमद्धर्मेश्वरदेवलब्धवरप्रसादेयुं, ईशपुररचितरामेश्वरप्रासादेयुं, विष्णुवर्धनमनोरागसागराभिवर्धनचन्द्रलेखेयुं, परिवारफलितकल्पकुजशाखेयुं, सदर्थसरससमयोचितवचनमधुरसस्यन्दिवदनारविन्देयुं, नगराजनन्दनापदारविन्दवन्दनवर्धितानन्देयुं, कलाकलापरत्नगर्भवसुन्धरेयुं, लावण्यसिन्धुवेलालीलायमानकेकरातिवन्धुरेयुं, भरतागमभवननिहितमहनीयमतिप्रदीपेयुं, विनयविनमद्विलासिनीकदम्बलम्बालकालम्बचरणनखकिरणकलापेयुं, दयारसामृतापूर्णवदनविधुबिम्बेयुं, अनूनदानाभिमानावलम्बेयुं, विचित्रनर्तनप्रवर्तनपात्रशिखामणियुं, सकलसमयरक्षामणियुं, सङ्गीतसङ्गतसरस्वतियुं, पतिविनयाविदितारुन्धतियुं, सवतिगन्धहस्तियुं, इत्यादिनामावलीप्रशस्तेयुमेनिसिद श्रीमत्पिरियरसि पट्टमहादेवि शान्तलदेवियर् वेरसु, श्रीमन्महापट्टणं वेलापुरद नेलेवीडिनोळ् श्रीमद्विष्णुवर्धनपोय्सळदेवर् सुखसङ्कथाविनोददिं राज्यं गेयुत्तमिर्दु ॥

स्वस्तिसमस्तमङ्गलाभ्युदयकरलक्षणलक्षितमुं, शब्दविद्ययंते सूत्रमुखसिद्धमुं, श्रुतिकदम्बदंते पदक्रमानुबद्धमुं, त्रिविक्रमावतारदंतिरुपक्रमप्रवृद्धमुं, चतुर्मुखनंते कमलोद्भवमुं, शशिखण्डमण्डननंते शिलापुत्रिकालङ्कृतमुं, शतक्रतुविनंते नयनाभिराममुं, कुलगिरियंते दृढमूलबन्धमुं,

जलाशयदंते कुमुदोल्लासियुं, मेरुगिरियंते बहुकनकघटितमुं, हरगिरियंते वृषपदाङ्कितमुं, गुरुवरणमागियुं तमोगुणमल्लदेयुं, स्तम्भसम्भृतमागियुं रजोगुणमल्लदेयुं, हर्षोत्कर्षकारियागियुं सत्वगुणमल्लदेयुं, सिंहगजावळियनुळ्ळुदागियुं गहनमल्लदेयुं, जलनिधियंते गभीरान्तरङ्गमुं, कनकशिखरियंते ध्रुवगतिनिरतमुं, चन्द्रमण्डलदंते सुधावलम्बियुं, रविमण्डलदंते वियत्पथवर्तियुं, गगनमण्डलदंते भगणसङ्क्रान्तमुं, बहुकूटकोटिघटितकलशविलासितमुं, बहुभूमिकोद्भासित श्रीमुखद्वारमुं, उत्तम्भितध्वजपटपल्लवोल्लङ्घ्यमानगगनवलयमुं, धराभारधौरिनागराज हृदयदर्शितगुरुत्वमुं, लब्धमहत्व .... मप्प श्रीमन्महाप्रासाददोळे ॥

स्वस्ति समस्तजगदुदयकरचतुरचतुराननोद्भूतिपूतपुण्डरीकदलधवळितोदरनुं, भुजबलानियुकहलमुखसमाकृष्टयमुनानदीप्रवाहविदितसामर्थ्यमुद्राभद्रबलभद्रसहोदरनुं, अमृतमथनसमयसंसिक्तसुव्यक्तबिन्दुवृन्दतारकितविकटवक्षःस्थलवियत्तलनुं, निजखुरघटितबिलगळितसकलजलधिजलकर्दमितपातालपङ्ककेळीविलोलवराहरूपहेलासमुत्तालितधरातलनुं, जगत्कण्टकोत्कण्ठदशकण्ठकण्ठकाण्डषण्डखण्डनप्रचण्डकाण्डमुखसमुद्भूतविजयविख्यातरामावतारनुं, धरणीभारावतारचितपाण्डवोपकारनुं, बलिकरनियुक्तधाराप्रवर्धमानवृद्धिलतारूढोद्दण्डपद्मजाण्डस्पृगाधारदण्डायमानकलेबरवरत्रिविक्रमावतारामितधरणीमण्डलनुं, अतिक्रूरदनुजाविनाशविरचितोपायरक्षिताखण्डलनुं, सुरासुरकराकृष्यमाणमन्दरभ्रमणभरसहातिधीरकमठाकारदर्शितदृढत्वनुं, परममहत्परिमाणगर्भीकृतसकलसत्वनुं, अज्ञातपरमार्थस्वरूपनागियुं प्रकटनुं, अनिकटीकृतनिकटनुं, अदूरीकृतदूरनुं, अतुङ्गीकृततुङ्गनुं, असूक्ष्मीकृतसूक्ष्मनुं, अगहनीकृतगहननुं, अनवनतगभीरनुं, अविस्तार्यमाणविस्तीर्णनुं, सकलभुवनसम्पूर्णनुं, संसारसमुचिततमःपटलविघटनप्रदीपनुं, परब्रह्मस्वरूपनुं, अतिप्रसन्ननुं, चेन्ननुमेनिप श्रीमद्विजयनारायणदेवरं श्रीमद्विष्णुवर्द्धनपोय्सळदेवर् सद्भक्तियिं सुप्रतिष्ठितं माडि ।

शकवर्ष सासिरद मूवत्तोंभत्तनेय हेमलम्बिसंवत्सरद चैत्रशुद्ध पञ्चमी वड्डवार श्रीविजयनारायणदेवर श्रीचेन्नकेशवदेवर श्रीलक्ष्मीनारायणदेवर नित्यनैमित्तिकदिव्याङ्गभोग त्रिकालनैवेद्य श्रीवैष्णवब्राह्मणर पात्रपागुड विद्यावंतर मालगाररारतिकोट्टणवोळगाद समस्त वूळिगद जीवितवर्गक्कवागि सर्वनमस्य समस्तकिरुकुळ देविदेवन काणकेसहित श्रीपाददल्लि धारापूर्वक माडिद वृत्ति वेलापुरद बीडु चतुःसीमे सुंकपोंनायसहित देवळिगेनाडेमेसंदिहन्नेरडु, आनाडिद वूर बसवनहळ्ळि, कोडगिनाड बारसि हन्नेरडु, निडुगुंद हळ्ळिगळु सहित, अब्बिदोरे तगरेनाडेरडु हसुडेहळ्ळिगळु सहित बळ्ळाविनाडहडियदवोळलु, अत्तिवळिगेय मणलिनाड मोरखुहन्नेरडु, नेक्कुनाड केसकोडुहळ्ळिगळु सहित मैसेनाड बेडगेरे आसंदिनाडेरडुं देवनूरु चतुस्सीमासहितं त्रिविक्रमं माडिद दिव्यश्रीपादपद्मंगळिगे समर्पिसिदरु ॥ इनितरिंद मिक्कधनमुं भक्तरायमुं खंडस्फुटितजीर्णोद्धारक्कवेकादशावतारनेनिसिद श्रीविष्णुवर्द्धनहोय्सळदेवर ॥

सामान्योऽयं धर्मसेतुर्नृपाणां काले काले पालनीयो भवद्भिः ।
सर्वानेतान् भाविनः पार्थिवेन्द्रान् भूयो भूयो याचते रामचन्द्रः ॥
स्वदत्तां परदत्तां वा यो हरेत वसुन्धराम् ।
षष्टिवर्षसहस्राणि विष्ठायां जायते क्रिमिः ॥
देवद्रव्यविनाशेन ब्रह्मस्वहरणेन च ।
तद्धनं कुलनाशाय भवेदात्मवधाय च ॥
॥ नारायणाय नमः ॥

Inscription on the pedestal of Vijaya-Narayana or Kesava.

1117

जिष्णुर्विष्णुमहीपालः पालिताखिलभूतलः ।
देवदेवेशविजयनारायणमचीकरत् ॥

Inscription on the pedastal of Kappe-Chennigaraya.

C 1117

शान्तिकृत्सर्वभूतानां प्रतिष्ठा विष्णुकान्तया ।
चेन्नकेशवदेवस्य शान्तिदेव्या कृतोत्तमा ॥
॥ पट्टमहादेवी ॥

Belur 20. 1180. (Extracts.)

स्वस्ति श्रीकुचकलशौ विशालमूलौ
दिश्यास्तामविरलचन्दनानुलेपौ ।
उत्तुङ्गौ हरिभुजकल्पवृक्षपुष्टिं
तन्वानौ मदनरसेन पूरितौ वः ॥
नारायणदेवर को । द्वारवनाकल्पमागे यक्षेशन भ ॥
ण्डारमेनल् माडिसिदनु । दारं बल्लाळदेवधरणीनाथं ॥
॥ श्रीकेशवाय नमः ॥

Belur, 72. C. 1185. (Extracts.)

आसीदेचलदेव्यां हि नारसिंहक्षितीश्वरात् ।
तस्यां पट्टमहादेव्यां बल्लाळः पृथिवीपतिः ॥
श्रीमच्छ्रीनरसिंहदेवनृपतेर्जातो महीयान् सुतः
सम्प्राप्तोरुपराक्रमो विजयते बल्लाळभूपालकः ।
हित्वा पापमहान्धकारमनिशं धर्मं समुद्दीपयन्
श्रीमत्केशवदेवपादयुगलध्यानामृतास्वादनः ॥
दशमुखभुजदण्डोद्घातकैलासशैलं
हर इव कलिवेगोच्चालितं धर्मजातम् ।
जगति बहुविधं यः स्थापयामास वीरः
स जयति रणमल्लो वीरबल्लाळभूपः ॥
जीयाद्बल्लाळभूपालः पालिताखिलभूतलः ।
यत्कीर्तिपुण्डरीकस्य पृथिवी कर्णिकायते ॥
एसेयल् जाळकजाळकं दृढकवाटं द्वारशाखालिबा
णसुकोट्टारखुदग्रवप्रमुदवासं वासुदेवाख्यती ।
र्थसरं श्रीविजयादिशब्दविलसन्नारायणंगोल्दु कल्
वेसर्दि तेङ्कणचक्रि माडिसिदनीबल्लाळभूपालकम् ॥

Belur 63. 1387.

स्वस्ति श्रीमच्छकाब्दे निधिगगनगुणक्ष्मामिते प्राभवाद्ये
मासे तत्पूर्णिमायां हरिहरनृपतौ मुद्दपे मन्त्रिवर्ये ।
शासत्युर्वीं च सर्वां मलगरसविभुः ख्यातकाश्मीरवंशः
प्रासादं केशवस्य स्फुटरुचिकलशेनाश्रयत्काञ्चनेन ॥
॥ १३०९ ॥

Belur 3. 1397. (Extracts.)

श्रीमत्त्रैलोक्यपूज्याय सर्वकर्मसुसाक्षिणे ।
फलदाय नमो नित्यं केशवाय शिवाय च ॥
एतत्सुरासुराधीशमौळिमालोपलालितम् ।

श्रीमद्वेलापुराधीशकेशवेशस्य शासनम् ॥

जम्बूद्वीपे परार्धे सकलगुणगणैर्भारते वर्षखण्डे
धामान्यत्युज्ज्वलानि त्रिदशमुनिगणैरार्चितान्यत्र सन्ति ।
देवानां पुण्यरूपाण्यपि शतमुचितं नाम तेषामथैतान्
वक्ष्ये कांश्चिद्यथार्हं सकृदिदमखिलं संशृणुध्वं च चित्रम् ॥

यं शैवास्समुपासते शिव इति ब्रह्मेति वेदान्तिनो
बौद्धा बुद्ध इति प्रमाणपटवः कर्तेति नैयायिकाः ।
अर्हन्नित्यथ जैनशासनमताः कर्मेति मीमांसकाः
सोऽयं वो विदधातु वाञ्छितफलं श्रीकेशवेशस्सदा ॥

सोऽयं पायादपायादपहसितसरोजातनेत्रान्तरश्री
राकल्पं कल्पवृक्षानिव विपुळकृपासारधाराधरो वः ।
लक्ष्मीवक्षोजशैलोपरि कपिशपटीविद्युदुद्योतमानः
श्रीवेलग्रामधामा निजपतिभवनाभाविताँ केशवो वः ॥

अरुणसरसिजश्रीसोदरैरत्युदारै
रखिळभुवनरक्षादीक्षितैर्दृष्टिपातैः ।
तरुणतुळसिमालालङ्कृतोरस्स्थळश्रीः
करुणयति कदा नः केशवेशः कृपेशः ॥

सर्वोत्कृष्टे समग्रैर्विविधगुणगणैः सत्वसारैकरम्ये
प्रख्याते होय्सळाख्ये महति जनपतेर्धाम्नि वेलानगर्याम् ।
आतन्वन्विष्णुदेवक्षितिपतिविभवान्विश्वरक्षाविधायी
योगं योगीन्द्रगम्यः कलयति कुशलं केशवो नाथ एषः ॥

अन्धान् व्यक्ताक्षिबन्धानलघुपरिणवद्राजमुद्रान् दरिद्रान्
पङ्गून् जङ्घालमुख्यानमरगुरुसदृग्वाक्समूकांश्च मूकान् ।
वन्ध्यास्सन्ततिबन्धुराश्च कलयन् देशान्यदेशागतान्
सर्वाभीष्टफलेन योजयति तान् वेलापुरीकेशवः ॥

संसारार्णवगर्ववारणकळावेळा हि वेलापुरी
मूर्तिस्त्वं प्रथमैव मूर्तिषु चतुर्विंशत्युपाख्यासु च ।
विष्णो नारदगीतवैभव हरे देवाधिदेवोत्तम
क्लेशध्वंसन सौम्यकेशव महालक्ष्मीपते पातु माम् ॥

श्रीमद्वेदान्तवेद्यादवचनविषयात्सच्चिदानन्दतत्वा

दाविर्भावं प्रपन्ने त्रिभुवनभवनेऽनादिमायाविचित्रे ।
अस्य स्थित्यै समर्थान्नृपकुलतिलकान् निर्ममे पद्मयोनिः
काले प्राप्ते कलौ तत्कलुषपरिहृतौ सङ्गमस्सान्वयोऽभूत् ॥
कूटस्थोऽभिजनस्य सङ्गमनृपः श्रीशारदासङ्गमा
ज्जाताः पञ्च सुरद्रुमा इव सुतास्तत्रादिमो हर्यपः ।
तस्यैका तनुरेव बुक्कनृपतिर्विश्वम्भरागोपति
स्तस्मादेष विवर्धते हरिहरः साम्राज्यलक्ष्मीवरः ॥
अर्यम्णस्तनुजो जनाय महते जाम्बूनदस्पर्शने
क्षोणीदानविधावसंशयमसौ श्रीरेणुकानन्दनः ।
इष्टापूर्तपरम्पराविरचने नान्योऽस्ति यस्योपमः
सोऽयं पुण्यमहीपतिर्हरिहरः श्रीमान् समुज्जृम्भते ॥
यद्वद्दशरथस्याभूत् सुमन्त्रस्सचिवो महान् ।
तद्वद्धरिहरस्य श्रीगुण्डदण्डाधिनायकः ॥
यद्दोर्दण्डप्रतापप्रबलतरमहावह्निवीर्यातिरेक
ज्वालामालापतङ्गायितयवनतुरुष्कान्ध्रशत्रुक्षितीशाः ।
सोऽयं बुद्धिप्रभावप्रगुणितनिजतेजोल्लसन्मन्त्रशक्तिः
मन्त्रिश्रेष्ठाग्रगण्यो जगति विजयते गुण्डदण्डाधिनाथः ॥
एतस्मिन् समरे विजित्य नृपतीन् प्रत्यर्थिनस्तद्वशू
कार्पण्येन विमुच्य तान् भुवमिमां धर्मेण संशासति ।
तस्याज्ञाकरणेषु मन्त्रिगुरुषु श्रीगुण्डदण्डाधिपः
प्राधान्येन विजृम्भते नृपकृतावंकप्रतापोज्ज्वलः ॥
अङ्गो व्यङ्गः कलिङ्गो विकळमतिरसौ गुर्जरस्सज्वरोऽभूत्
पञ्चाळाः पञ्चभावं दधति बहुबलः सैन्धवः सिन्धुपाती ।
आन्ध्रोऽप्यन्धः प्रबद्धश्चटुलभटवदुक्षिप्तनासीरपार्श्वे
श्चोळः कौळत्वमाप स्मरति रणरसं गुण्डदण्डाधिनाथे ॥
अङ्गः सङ्गरभङ्गितो रणमहारङ्गं कलिङ्गो जहा
वन्ध्रः पर्वतरन्ध्रगस्समजहाद्दुर्जेस्वरं गूर्जरः ।
कोणं कोङ्कणकोटका जगुरगाच्चोळोऽपि शैलान्तरम्
श्रीमद्गुण्डचमूपतौ सकलसेनापत्यसंस्थे सति ॥
स्वस्ति श्रीमदशेषमन्त्रिवरविख्यातातिशौर्यातिगा

म्भीर्यौदार्यसुधैर्यवीर्यविजयश्रीकीर्तिनित्योदयः ।
भूधर्मद्विजदेववेदकुलरक्षादुष्टशिक्षाकरः
पुण्योदर्कचरित्रकोऽस्तदुरितः श्रीगुण्डदण्डाधिपः ॥
यत्प्रत्योघविदारितारिधरणीपालावनारोद्धृत
स्त्रीरत्नच्छलवैरिवीरविजयश्रीकौतुकोत्साहितम् ।
श्रीमद्वीरहरीन्द्रराजमनिशं कुर्वन्नवावोत्तम
प्रायानीकगणाधिनाथविजयश्रीगुण्डदण्डाधिपः ॥
यद्वाटीपुटघोटकव्रजखुरक्षुण्णक्षमामण्डलो
द्भूतस्फीतदिगन्तरावृतरजो राजन्नभोमण्डले ।
प्रत्यर्थिक्षितिपालसंस्थविजयश्रीकौतुकं गुण्डद
ण्डाधीशस्य विधातुमन्तरितवस्त्राकारमुज्जृम्भते ॥
अग्रे यद्गणना प्रवीरपरिषद्गोष्ठीषु काष्ठां गता
प्रख्यातिः प्रतिजन्यमूर्जितजयश्रीपाणिपीडाविधिः ।
यत्ते गुण्डपदण्डनाथ निबिडो भावस्सदा त्र्यम्बके
सर्वं चैतदुदारहरिहरनृपश्रीपादपद्मप्रभा ॥
रामस्येव स मारुतिर्हरिहरक्षोणीपतेरग्रणी
र्भृत्यो गुण्डपदण्डनाथसुभटो लङ्कामिव स्कन्दयन् ।
जित्वा केरळतौळवान्ध्रकुटकानानीय तेभ्यः श्रियं
राज्ञे सम्प्रददाति मन्त्रिनृपयोस्तत्सामरस्यं परम् ॥
वेतण्डानिव सैपपाथेयमुखान्मत्तान् तुरुष्कान् रणे
केशेष्वेव निगृह्य वाजिभवने शाखामृगाः कारिताः ।
अन्यौ ज्येष्ठकनिष्ठसञ्ज्ञकमहाव्याघ्रौ गृहीतौ गळे
श्रीमद्गुण्डपदण्डनाथ भवते तिष्ठेत कस्स्पर्धया ॥
सन्तापाख्यमिरम्मदं ज्वलयति स्वान्तेष्वहङ्कारिणां
सान्द्रं वर्षति वैरिवृन्दरुधिरं यत्खड्गकालाम्बुदे ।
धत्ते साधुकदम्बमुत्सवदशां कीर्ति नवं केतकी
सौरभ्यं भजते दिशासु विजयश्रीगुण्डदण्डाधिपः ॥
इदं विजयते पुरो भवनभूषणं शार्ङ्गिणः
सुमेरुहिमसानुमन्मलयमन्दरप्रक्रियम् ।
त्रिविष्टपपदोन्नमच्छिखरचारु सिद्धाङ्गना
पदाम्बुजपरिस्खलत्कनकनूपुरं गोपुरम् ॥

Belur 13. 1484. (Extracts.)

अष्टे प्राप्तो मधुवनृपतेस्तेन मागाम्बिकायां
लब्धक्ष्माभृन्मणिरिव महान्वारिधेस्ताम्रपर्ण्याम् ।
यः सद्भक्त्या गुणगणनिधिः केशवाराधनार्थं
भद्रा लक्ष्मीभवनविभवा कारिता यागशाला ॥
इयमाचन्द्रार्कं स्थिरा भवतु ॥

Belur 11. C. 1484. (Extracts.)

लब्धक्षोणीचक्रकीर्त्या विधुविधु . . स्यैरावतस्वच्छमूर्त्या
जाते चान्द्रे करण्डे बहुवृषजनुषा पुण्डरीकोद्भवाण्डे ।
दुग्धाब्धिर्दैत्यहन्त्रामलविबुधधुनी भ्रभ्रजालोद्गतौघैः
श्रीकण्ठः कण्ठकान्त्या निभृत इव जनैर्लक्ष्मणा ज्ञायते ग्लौः ॥

Belur 64. 1736.

श्रीमत्पुण्ये शकाब्दे ग्रहशररसभूसम्मिते नालनैज
ज्येष्ठे तत्कृष्णपक्षप्रभ्यसमगुरुदिने कृष्णभूपे च सौम्ये ।
नञ्जाख्ये राज्ञि शासत्यखिलभुवमसौ वेङ्कटाख्यो नृपालः
प्रासादं केशवस्य स्थिरकलशयुतं कारयामास दिव्यम् ॥
॥ १६५९ ॥

Belur 65. 1774.

श्रीमद्रम्ये शकाब्दे नगनिधिरसभूगण्यमाने जयाख्ये
द्वादश्यां शुक्लपक्षे नभसि गुरुदिने चामराजे नृपाले ।
शासत्युर्वीं नवाबप्रवरबहदरे हैदरल्याख्यभूपे
प्रासादं केशवस्य स्थिरकलशयुतं नञ्जयार्यो व्यतानीत् ॥
॥ १६९७ ॥

By the same author.

ARCHITECTURE AND SCULPTURE IN MYSORE, No. 1.

THE KESAVA TEMPLE AT SOMANATHAPUR.

(*On sale by the Curator, Government Book Depot, Bangalore.*)

EXTRACTS FROM OPINIONS OF SCHOLARS AND THE PRESS.

The printing, paper and half-tone plates all are of the best quality, and the account of the building and sculptures is adequate. The publication does credit to all concerned.—*Dr. Vincent A. Smith, M. A., C. I. E.*

Both the contents and the attractive get-up of the book make it a most welcome publication to all lovers of ancient Indian art.—*Dr. J. Ph. Vogel.*

It was a happy idea to issue these descriptions separately, and the result is admirably successful.—*Dr. L. D. Barnett.*

It is an excellent work both on the architectural, and also on the historical and archæological, side. The plates and photographs are admirable. The illustrations of signed works of art are a most interesting feature. Your past and present researches in this line will some day lead to a biographical history of Indian art (at least for some periods and areas). I hope that the Series will be maintained with the same success which has attended the 'Government Oriental Library Sanskrit Series', with great credit to the State.—*Dr. F. W. Thomas.*

The illustrations are beyond all praise and could not be surpassed.—*Mr. L. Rice, C.I.E*

The great archæological wealth of the State of Mysore is only now coming to light, thanks to the labours of Mr. R. Narasimhachar, M. A., M. R. A. S., who, under encouragement of the enlightened Government of the State, has taken in hand a systematic study of the ancient monuments in which the country abounds. A few of them have been briefly referred to before in the works of Fergusson, of Mr. and Mrs. Workman and of Mr. Rice in his volumes of the Epigraphia Carnatica. More detailed accounts are now appearing in the annual Archæological Reports of Mysore, and the State has further arranged to issue a few special short monographs, fully illustrated, of the more notable structures of the Hoysala and Dravidian types dealing in some detail with both the architecture and sculpture of the buildings. It is contemplated later to prepare a complete monograph on Hoysala architecture in Mysore. The first of the short monographs referred to is on the Kesava temple at Somanathapur, a photograph of which we reproduce from the monograph. It is a typical structure of the period, possessed of great beauty and in a good state of preservation.—*Indian Engineering.*

Rao Bahadur Narasimhachar has undertaken to issue about half a dozen short monographs, with suitable illustrations, on the notable buildings of the Hoysala and Dravidian styles. The present monograph on the well known Kesava temple is the first of the Series. The printing of the text and the illustrations has been very neatly executed by the Mysore Government Press at Bangalore.

The illustration of the two towers which Mr. Narasimhachar gives fully bears out the praise bestowed on them by Workman in his *Through Town and Jungle*. The illustrations of images and inner details (which are accessible only to a Hindu writer) bring us in closer touch with the temple. Many of the images are signed by the artists. The image of Venu-Gopala is the most elegant of the illustrated specimens. The exquisite ceilings would furnish fine models for modern buildings.—*Indian Antiquary*.

We are glad to note that the Government of Mysore have begun to adopt the suggestion which we have on many occasions made in our columns in reviewing the progress of the Archæological Survey of Mysore on the desirability of issuing monographs on individual works of sculptural and architectural merit with which the State abounds. The first monograph of the proposed Mysore Archæological Series is devoted to the Kesava temple at Somanathapur. The temple, which dates back to the 13th century, is a splendid example of the Hoyṣala style of temple architecture. Rao Bahadur R. Narasimhachar, the author of the monograph, has embodied in it many photo-plates giving various views of this admirable temple on which generations of the best Indian artisans of old appear to have lavished their technical and artistic skill. There is a complete account of the temple, traditional and historical, as well as based on the inscriptions copied from the temple, given in the monograph. We are glad that what has been successfully attempted and carried out in the case of the Somanathapur temple is to be done in the case of numerous other temples in the State, the historical importance and structural merits of which have attracted the attention and the admiration of antiquarians all the world over.—*Madras Mail*.

We cannot sufficiently praise Mr. R. Narasimhachar for his indefatigable exertions in the exploration of the artistic treasures of Mysore. The annual Administration Reports of the Archæological Survey of Mysore published under his superintendence have for a long time been famous for their varied interest and the wealth of information they contain, and have rightly attracted the attention of scholars both in and outside India. Mr. Narasimhachar has thought it right to publish a series of monographs on the different kinds of architecture in Mysore. The first of the series is entitled the "Kesava temple at Somanathapur". The temple is of extraordinary beauty both from the architectural and sculptural point of view. To give a true idea of the size, construction and artistic beauty of the temple to those who have not actually seen it one should reproduce all that is written in the monograph. We recommend its study to all lovers of History and Art.—*United India and Native States*.

A detailed description is given of the temple, its dimensions, its sculptures, its inscriptions. Twenty-three unusually good reproductions from photographs illustrate the text. Special congratulation is due to Mr. T. Namassivayam Pillai, who prepared them. We have also a ground plan of the temple, a summary of the contents of the main inscriptions, and the Samskrit text of those parts of the inscriptions which are written in that language.—*New India*.

The charming volume before us is the first of the Mysore Archæological Series: *Architecture and Sculpture in Mysore* and has appeared not a day too soon. It is a matter of no small gratification to us to welcome the present volume which is sumptuously provided with photos of all that is best and most interesting in the supremely beautiful and captivating edifice at Somanathapur. No one who studies the illustrations in the book can fail to feel increased pride for the country which possesses such treasures and for the race which produced such artists. Indeed books of this kind help to fan the fire of patriotism and quicken national revival, and we cannot be too grateful to Mr. Narasimhachar for the very valuable volume he has presented to his countrymen. We hope that the Mysore Government will make it possible for him to bring out quickly the other volumes of the Series.—*Mythic Society's Journal*.

PLATE I

Mysore Archaeological Survey

SOUTH VIEW OF BUILDINGS IN THE ENCLOSURE OF KESAVA TEMPLE AT BELUR

Pl. II.

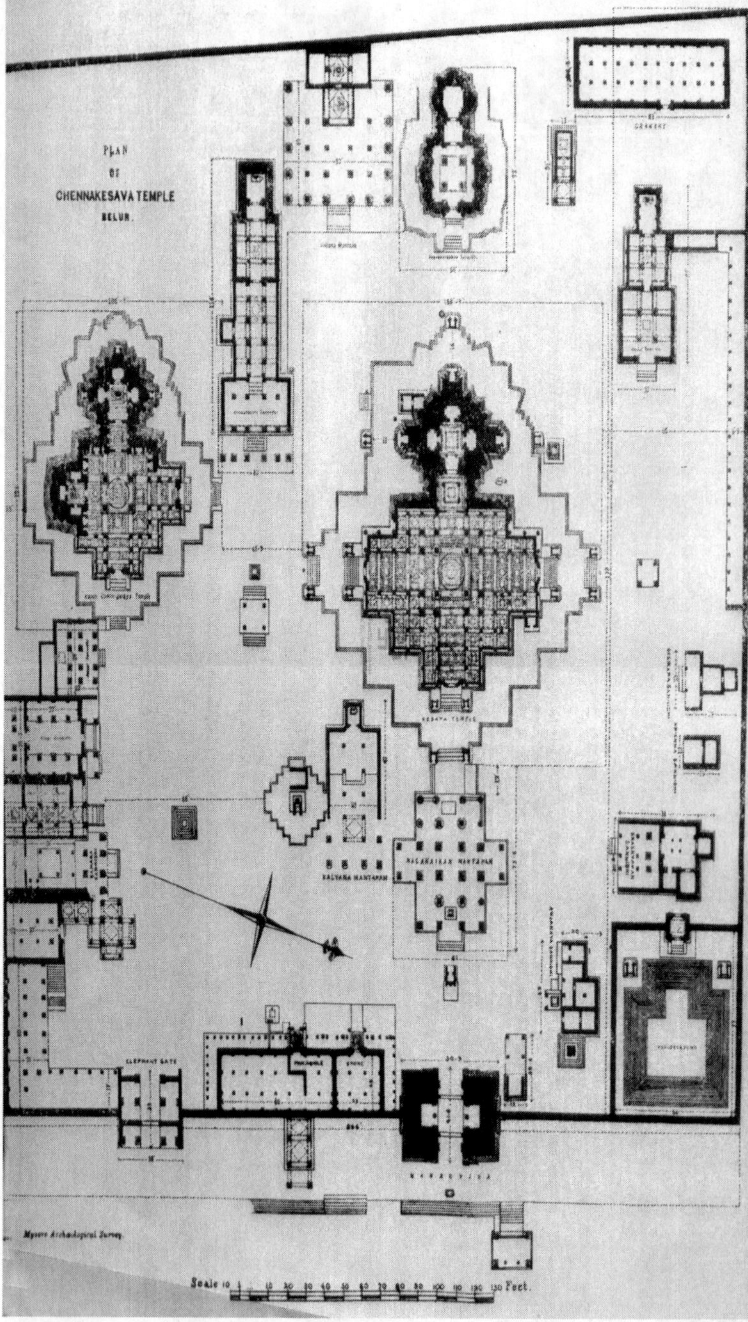
PLAN
OF
CHENNAKESAVA TEMPLE
BELUR.
ELEPHANT GATE
KALYANA MANTAPAM
Mysore Archaeological Survey.
Scale 10 5 0 10 20 30 40 50 60 70 80 90 100 110 120 130 Feet.

PLATE III

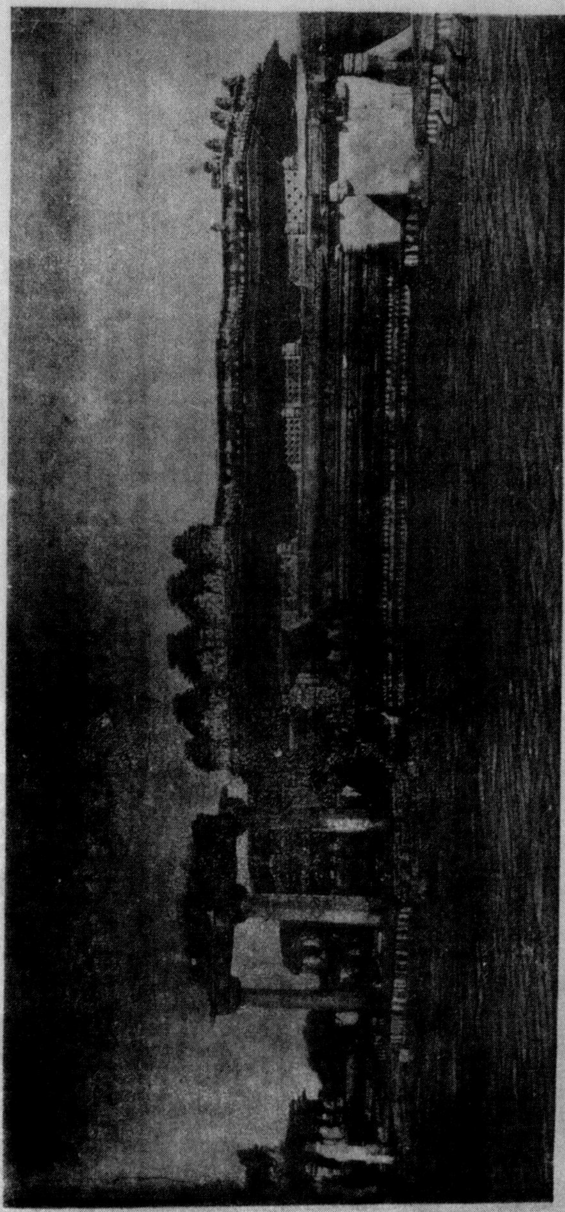

SOUTH VIEW OF KESAVA TEMPI

PLATE IV

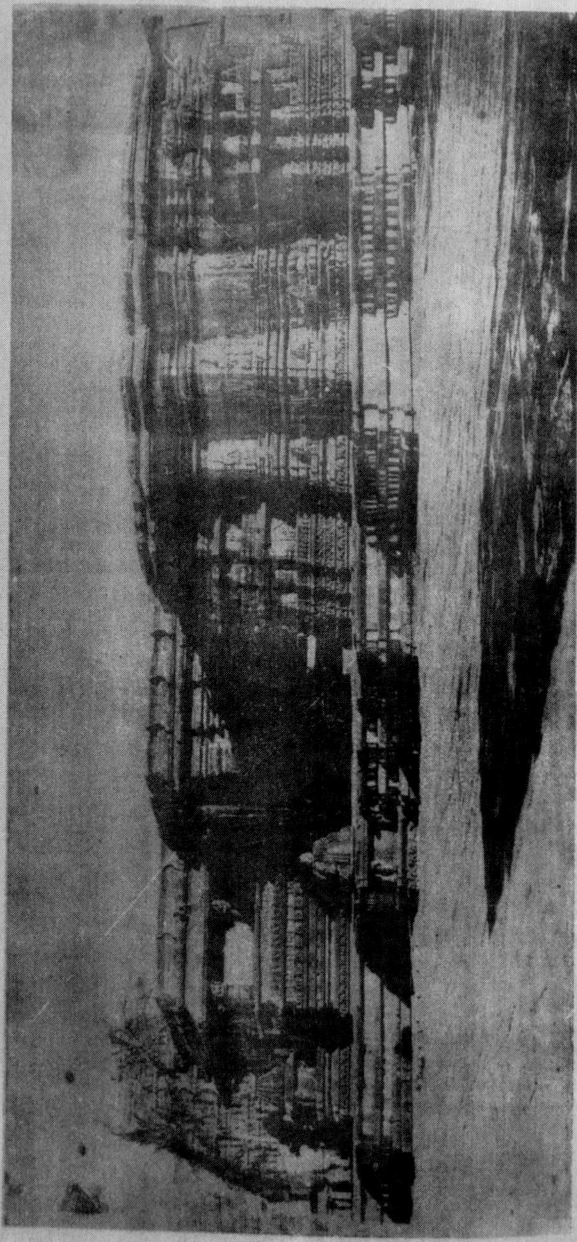

NORTH VIEW OF KESAVA TEMPLE

Mysore Archæological Survey]

PLATE V

EAST ENTRANCE

PLATE VI

NORTH ENTRANCE

EAST DOORWAY OF THE KESAVA TEMPLE. Pl. VII.

Mysore Archaeological Survey.

PLATE VIII

RAILED PARAPET ON THE SOUTH WALL

Mysore Archæological Survey]

PLATE IX

RAILED PARAPET ON THE SOUTH WALL, ENLARGED, OMITTING BOTTOM FRIEZE.

(Mysore Archæological Survey)

SCREEN. GEOMETRICAL DESIGN.

Pl. X.

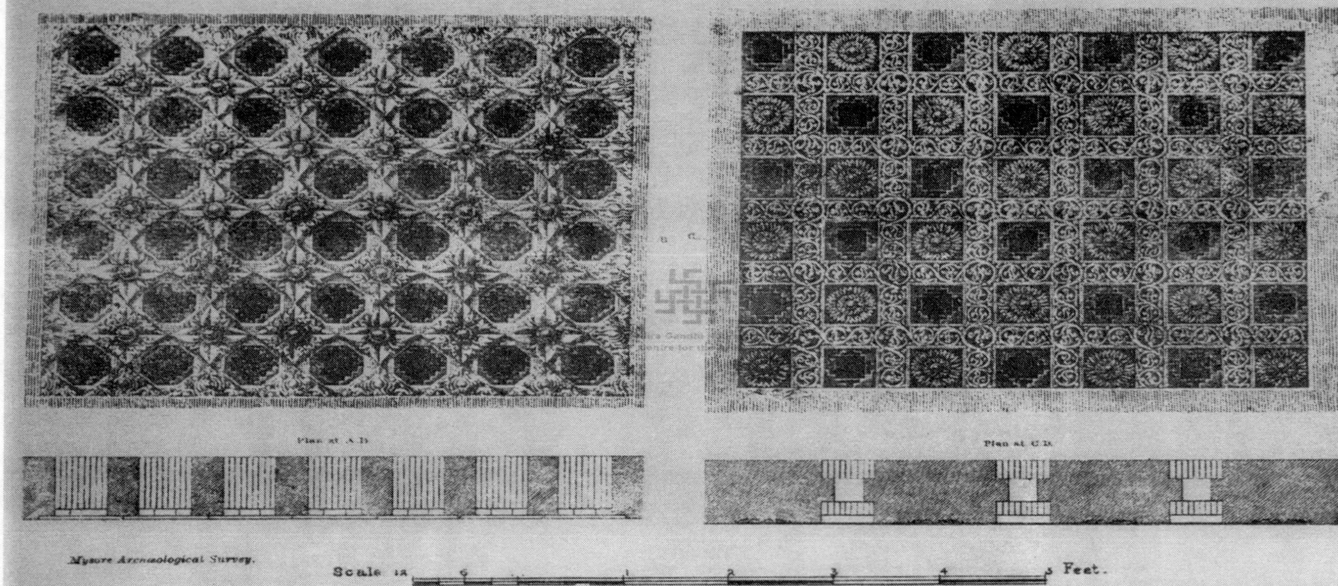

Mysore Archaeological Survey.

Pl. XI.

SCREEN GEOMETRICAL DESIGN.

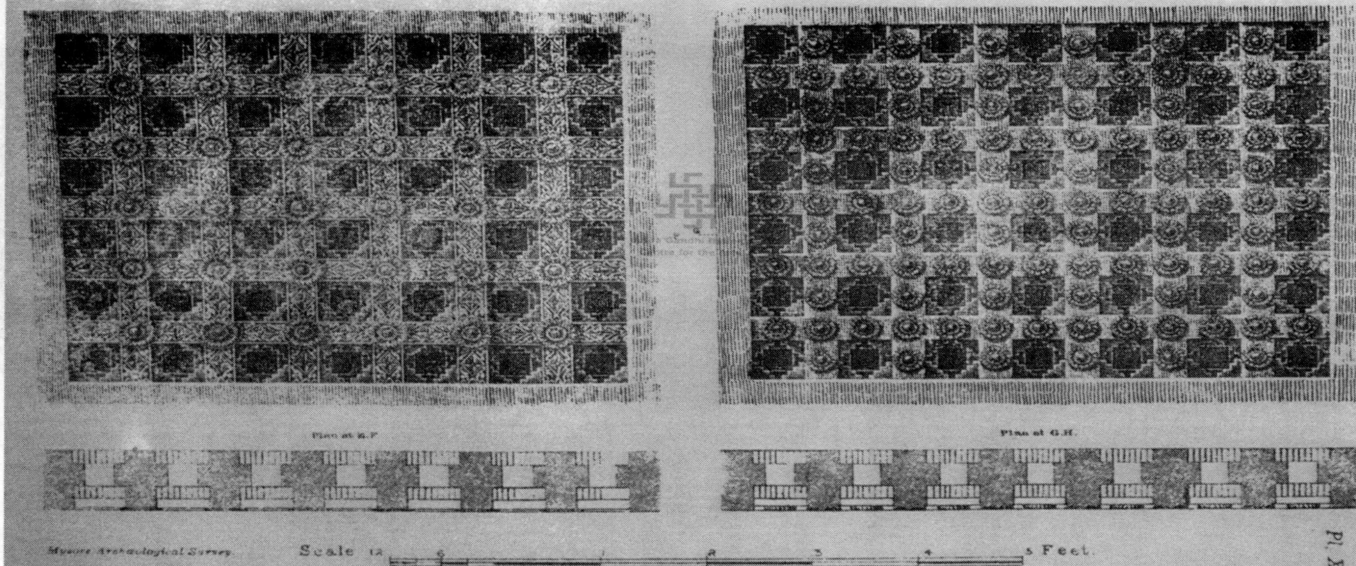

Mysore Archaeological Survey.

PLATE XII

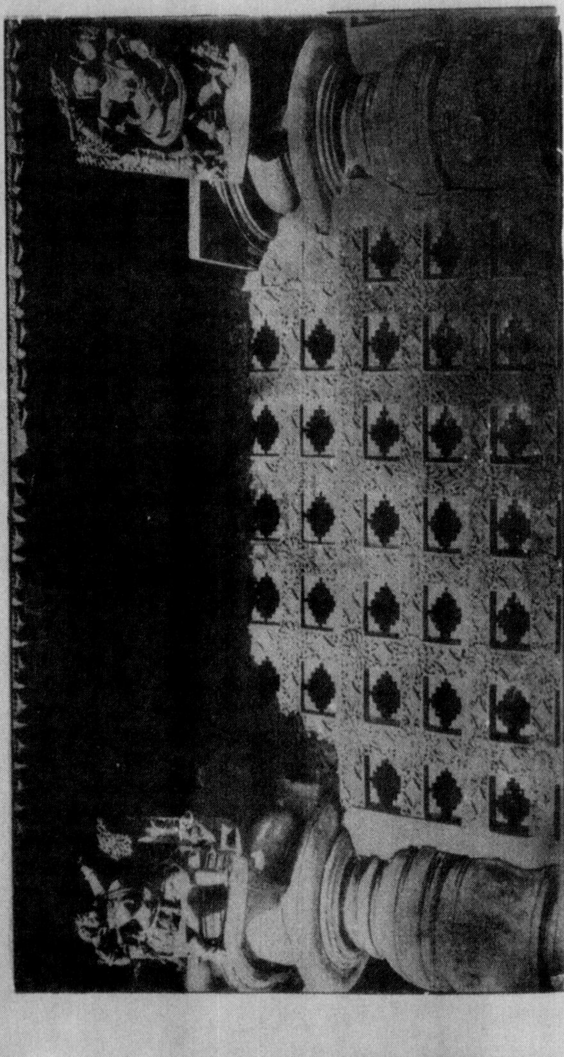

SCREEN, GEOMETRICAL DESIGN

Mysore Archaeological Survey]

SCULPTURED SCREEN, DARBAR OF VISHNUVARDHNA

Mysore Archæological Survey]

PLATE XIV

SCULPTURED SCREEN, STORY OF PRAHLADA

Mysore Archæological Survey]

PLATE XV

SCULPTURED SCREEN, DARBAR OF NARASIMHA I

Mysore Archæological Survey]

PLATE XVI

Mysore Archæological Survey] SIX MADANAKAI OR BRACKET FIGURES

PLATE XVII

Mysore Archaeological Survey

FOUR LARGE IMAGES ON THE WEST WALL

PLATE XVIII

Mysore Archæological Survey]

NORTH CAR-LIKE NICHE

PLATE XIX

FRONT VIEW OF PAVILION TO LEFT OF EAST ENTRANCE

Mysore Archæological Survey]

PLATE XX

SIDE VIEW OF PAVILION TO RIGHT OF EAST ENTRANCE.

Mysore Archæological Survey]

SUKHANASI DOORWAY

Mysore Archaeological Survey.

PLATE XXII

INTERIOR OF NAVARANGA OR MIDDLE HALL.

PLATE XXIII

TWO PILLARS ON THE VERANDAS OF MIDDLE HALL

Mysore Archaeological Survey

PLATE XXIV

THE NARASIMHA PILLAR IN MIDDLE HALL

Mysore Archæological Survey]

PLATE XXV

ANOTHER PILLAR IN MIDDLE HALL

Mysore Archæological Survey

PLATE XXVI

PORTION OF CENTRAL CEILING OF MIDDLE HALL

Mysore Archæological Survey]

BRACKET FIGURE ON SOUTH-EAST PILLAR OF MIDDLE HALL

Mysore Archæological Survey]

PLATE XXVIII

BRACKET FIGURE ON SOUTH-WEST PILLAR OF MIDDLE HALL.

Mysore Archaeological Survey]

BRACKET FIGURE ON NORTH-EAST PILLAR OF MIDDLE HALL.

Mysore Archæological Survey]

PLATE XXX

BRACKET FIGURE ON NORTH-WEST PILLAR OF MIDDLE HALL

Mysore Archæological Survey]

CEILING IN FRONT OF EAST ENTRANCE

Mysore Archæological Survey]

PLATE XXXII

SIGNED IMAGES

ADHARASAKTI EXECUTED BY BHANDARI-MADHUVANNA

VENUGOPALA, EXECUTED BY MADHUVANNA

Mysore Archaeological Survey.

PLATE XXXIII

EAST VIEW OF KAPPE-CHENNIGARAYA TEMPLE

Mysore Archæological Survey]

Pl. XXXIV. SUKHANASI DOORWAY OF KAPPE-CHENNIGARAYA TEMPLE.

Mysore Archæological Survey.

PLATE XXXV

MAHISHASURAMARDINI IN KAPPE-CHENNIGARAYA TEMPLE

Mysore Archaeological Survey]

Pl. XXXVI. CEILING, IN KAPPE-CHENNIGARAYA TEMPLE.

Mysore Archæological Survey.

Scale 12 6 1 2 3 4 5 Feet.

CEILING IN KAPPE CHENNIGARAYA TEMPLE. Pl. XXXVII.

Mysore Archæological Survey.

Scale 12 6 1 2 3 4 Feet.

PLATE XXXVIII

VISHNUVARDHANA AND SANTALE

Mysore Archaeological Survey]

Mysore Archæological Survey]

EAST VIEW OF VIRA-NARAYANA TEMPLE

PLATE XL

LAKSHMI-NARAYANA ON SOUTH WALL OF ANDAL TEMPLE

Mysore Archæological Survey)

PLATE XLI

LAKSHMI-NARAYANA ON SOUTH WALL OF ANDAL TEMPLE

Pl. XLII.

CEILING IN FRONT OF THE STOREHOUSE.

Mysore Archaeological Survey.

Scale 12 6 1 2 3 4 Feet.